F-15 EAGLE

Previous page: F-15A of the 555th TFTS, 58th TTW starting up and taxying out. The 'Triple Nickel', with a famous Vietnam War record, was the first squadron in the USAF to get the Eagle. *USAF*

Below: March 1978 – the 49th TFW begins to get its Eagles during 'Ready Holloman' as an F-15A breaks ground at Luke AFB, Arizona. *USAF*

F-15 EAGLE

Modern Combat Aircraft 12

Jeff Ethell

LONDON
IAN ALLAN LTD

Cover: Eagles on patrol. *USAF*

First published 1981
Reprinted 1984

ISBN 0 7110 1073 0

United States distribution by

Motorbooks International
Publishers & Wholesalers Inc
Osceola, Wisconsin 54020, USA ®

Published by Ian Allan Ltd, Shepperton, Surrey; and printed by Ian Allan Printing Ltd at their works at Coombelands in Runnymede, England.

Contents

Acknowledgements

With an airplane as complex as the F-15 Eagle it would have been impossible to write this book without the help of a great many experts on the airplane as well as many men in the Service itself who have been intimately involved with the original development and operational deployment of the US Air Force's primary fighter.

James P. Stevenson, himself an accomplished aviation writer and author of *McDonnell Douglas F-15 Eagle,* published by Aero Publishers, has been a constant help throughout my struggle to put the aircraft's history and capabilities in perspective. Not only was he a constant supplier of firsthand source material, but he was also able to advise and direct my interest into several areas of the aircraft's hidden recesses. In the process Jim has become a close friend and fellow traveller into the world of aviation history.

John Dennison, John McGrath, Lon Nordeen, John J. Burns and N. Gordon LeBert at the McDonnell Aircraft Company in St Louis, not only hosted me during my trip to McDonnell Douglas, but provided a constant stream of photographs and information on the Eagle. Without their support and encouragement, this look at an amazing airplane would have been very shallow indeed.

Lt-Col Stephen B. Hinderliter and Capt Gary B. Hoffman at Tactical Air Command's Office of Public Affairs put their support behind obtaining needed information in regard to the F-15 in service, from small details to visiting F-15 units.

Brig-Gen Jerry Dalton, Director of Information for the Secretary of the Air Force, put his usual support behind the project as he has done on numerous occasions in the past.

Maj Paul K. Kahl, Sr, Chief of the Magazine and Books Division of the Air Force, was instrumental in providing extensive information and photography on the Eagle from seemingly innumerable requests. Paul was continually making himself available to help, as were his Public Affairs Officers around the globe.

John Boyd and Pierre Sprey who were involved in formulating the concepts that led to the F-15, made themselves continually available for interviews, criticism and questions. It is their impressions that form the basis of how the F-15 came about.

Barry Watts and Chuck Spinney in the Pentagon took invaluable time to keep the real world of fighter aviation evident throughout the manuscript.

Jim Lynch, Larry Rogers and John L. Jones at Pratt & Whitney Aircraft in Florida supplied a wealth of information on the F100 engine, from origin to current use.

An unforgettable trip to RAF Alconbury, England, to fly in the F-15 with the 36th Tac Fighter Wing was made possible through Lt-Col Ronald L. Sherman, Chief of the Public Information Division, United States Air Forces in Europe. On arrival at Alconbury, Capt Ron Hinkle, Information Officer for the 10th Tactical Reconnaissance Wing, introduced me to Col Perry Smith, 36th Wing Commander, and Lt-Col Dick Stamm, 22nd Squadron Commander, who flew me in the Eagle. That flight will remain a most unforgettable experience.

William Heimdahl, Jacob Neufeld, Capt Don Rightmyer, Larry Paszek, and Lt-Col John A. Phillips of the Office of Air Force History made every effort to provide what was needed in the way of research and criticism on F-15 history, a challenge for all since most of the information was classified and had to be down-graded for public use.

To all of you, my deepest thanks.

1. 'Mr Mac' and the Company

The McDonnell Douglas fighter factory in St Louis, Missouri and one of its major products the F-15, bear the indelible stamp of founder James Smith McDonnell, the youngest son of a well-to-do cotton farmer in Little Rock, Arkansas. According to his older brother, William, James McDonnell was rather shy, serious and withdrawn with a penchant for hard work inherited from his Scottish father, who insisted that his sons earn all their own spending money.

McDonnell went to Princeton University, Class of 1921, and worked in the dining hall for pocket money, while studying physics so doggedly that he had little time for social life. The one frivolity he spent his money on was $10.00 for an aerial tour of the campus in a rickety old biplane in the fall of 1917 prior to classes. He then proceeded to go without a new winter overcoat. According to his freshman roommate, Edward L. Barbee, 'He didn't mingle or mix with people, he always was a one idea man. One time he spent a whole week in his room deciding that he believed that there was really a God.'

While at Princeton, McDonnell made a decision to specialise in aeronautical engineering. At the same time his interest turned abidingly toward the occult, and McDonnell's products have reflected that in taking names from the spirit world. His approaches to business were already detached, deliberate and precise. He had worked out a 50-year plan for his career and he juggled the details to fit aviation, deciding among other things 'to intern until age 40 before making a serious attempt to set up my own company.'

Pursuing his plan methodically he earned a master's degree in aeronautical engineering from MIT, Class of 1925. Two years earlier he had enlisted in the Army Reserve to learn to fly. He remembered singing hallelujahs during his first solo aerobatics. He also recalled 'something like psychic ecstasy during my first parachute jump. The ecstasy ended when I landed in weeds and gravel and the open chute pulled me through them.'

Mac was so intense with his new found profession that he even attempted to work for aircraft manufacturers for nothing, but in time he managed to land a $108 a month draftsman job at Huff Daland Airplane Company. Later he became a stress analyst at Buffalo's Consolidated Aircraft Company, but before long he was politely asked to look for employment elsewhere. Going on to Ford Motor Company's Aviation Division he was soon fired outright.

Undaunted, McDonnell decided if he couldn't find employment with people who appreciated his talent, he would develop his own airplane for the Guggenheim Safe Aircraft Award in 1929. The prize was $100,000, enough to help him advance his own projects. Unfortunately, on two attempts the aircraft failed to win the prize.

This didn't stop McDonnell. He later went to work for the Glenn L. Martin Company, where he ended up becoming the Chief Project Engineer for land planes, and in 1939 with $165,000 put together from his own savings, plus investments squeezed out of family, friends and others, he started McDonnell Aircraft in a $100 a month second story room at Lambert Field in St Louis. McDonnell had just turned 40 when he moved into those offices. He was right on schedule.

When asked why he waited so long before deciding to form his own company, he replied, 'When I was a young man I heard the first Henry Ford say, no man should start his own business until he's 40 because no man has enough experience to start a new business until he reaches that age.' The total number of employees – two; himself and a male secretary. But being a thrifty Scotsman, 'Mr Mac' rented part of his space to a group of Navy fliers and squeezed his own desks and drafting tables into a corner behind the fliers' canvas cots, mosquito netting and dirty underwear.

Three months after incorporation, engineering employment stood at 15. The first manufacturing order was for $7,672 worth of small parts for Stinson observation planes. In September 1940, the Company received a $20,000 Army Air Corps contract for jet propulsion research and in December of that year, McDonnell Aircraft was awarded its first major sub-contract for the manufacture of aircraft parts. Some of those parts were for the C-47 built by Douglas, the Company with which McDonnell would later merge.

In September 1941 McDonnell won an Army Air Force contract for the XP-67 twin engined propeller-

Left: 'Mr Mac's' first major design contract was with the USAAF during World War 2 for the twin-engined XP-67. With rare exceptions, McDonnell's fighters, from the beginning, have had two powerplants. *MCAIR*

Below: The first Phantom, the FH-1, in front of McDonnell Aircraft's first headquarters building in St Louis, Mo in the late 1940s. *MCAIR*

Left: The FH-1 Phantom was the first US jet fighter to operate from an aircraft carrier, leading to a long line of twin-engined jet fighters from the McDonnell plant in St Louis. *MCAIR*

driven bomber destroyer, the first experimental aircraft of all-McDonnell design conceived to obtain a maximum speed of 405mph, with a combat range of 2,385 statute miles. Only one experimental plane was flight tested but fell short of its design goal. 'Mr Mac' looked back on the XP-67 as something of a frustration since he was adamant about producing only successful projects.

The major contract that floated McDonnell for World War 2 was a production contract for producing all-wood AT-21 twin engined bomber crew trainers. They were manufactured from Fairchild designs at a McDonnell operated plant in Memphis, Tennessee.

In 1943 the contract came that turned the fortunes of the McDonnell Aircraft Company. That contract was for the US Navy's first carrier-based jet aircraft. It was a fortunate break and 'Mr Mac' liked to point out, 'It didn't come by chance.' It came because of McDonnell's earlier Army Air Force contract in jet propulsion. He had tried to interest the Navy previously in a contract to build a jet aircraft, but they didn't see the potential at that time. 'Mr Mac' recalled, 'It was on New Year's Eve, I was sitting in my office and it was well into the evening when I got this call from a Rear Admiral in the Bureau of Aeronautics. I remember being favourably impressed that the Navy was working that late in Washington. The Admiral said, "If you will be here tomorrow at 8.00am we can tell you about a classified item I think you will be interested in." I said, "Will do", and headed there overnight. When they told me what it was all about, I said, "Will do" again and then I came back and we went to work.'

Two years later the twin jet, single seat XFD-1 (later FH-1) Phantom as it was officially known, became the Navy's first aircraft to attain 500mph. It flew for the first time on 26 January 1945, the first in an historic series of twin-engined fighter aircraft for which McDonnell has become renowned.

On 21 July 1946 the Phantom proved its operational capability when it made a normal take-off and landing on the USS *Franklin D. Roosevelt.* This was the first time a combat jet aircraft had operated from the flight deck of an aircraft carrier.

Total sales at the end of World War 2 had come to $57,070,712. By 1947 the F2H Banshee had been ordered and by mid-1948 this aircraft was being developed in day fighter, night fighter and photo reconnaissance versions. The first production version of the Banshee was delivered to the fleet in 1949 and a total of 895 Banshees were finally built. This aircraft served in the Korean War as one of the Navy's major fighters.

At about the same time McDonnell engineers were developing the Banshee another group of engineers started advance design of the large XF-88 intended to be a long range supersonic bomber escort/penetration fighter for the Air Force, first flown in 1948. This design eventually grew into the larger F-101 Voodoo, used by three major US Air Force Commands; Strategic, Tactical and Air Defense. Three versions – long range attack fighter, interceptor and photo reconnaissance – accounted for a total production of 807 Voodoos. The 101 is still operational with Air National Guard squadrons in the US and with the Canadian Armed Forces.

In January 1949 long before the last Banshee was off the ramp at St Louis, development started on the F3H Demon, a single engine, all-weather carrier-based fighter. The Demon had serious engine and

Left: The F2H Banshee saw distinguished service in the Korean War, becoming quite popular with its pilots. *MCAIR*

Below: One of 'Mr Mac's' rare gambles in single-engine fighters was the F3H Demon – it never was very successful due primarily to engine problems. *MCAIR*

weight problems which were ameliorated but never solved. During this period there were several odd aircraft that McDonnell produced, including the XF-85 Goblin 'parasite' fighter, several different helicopter projects and later there was a project to produce a corporate business jet that had four engines.

Certainly the McDonnell fortunes came to a highpoint in the development of the Phantom II. In the summer of 1953 McDonnell's engineers began preliminary design on a new jet, then known to the Navy as the F3H-G project study. By November 1954 the aircraft went through another re-designation as the single seat AH-1 attack aircraft, which became known under Navy funding as the F4H-1, a supersonic, twin engine, twin seat, fleet defence interceptor.

On 27 May 1958, the XF4H-1 made its first flight from Lambert St Louis International Airport. By December 1960 the Phantom had joined the fleet and then in the early 1960s proceeded to set a number of world records. After entering Navy and Marine Corps fighter and reconnaissance squadrons, it wasn't long before the efficiency-minded Secretary of Defense, Robert McNamara, was thinking of forcing the reluctant USAF to buy it. Indeed, the Air Force, despite its preference of the nuclear strike F-105, proceeded to make its first buy in 1962. The British Royal Navy and Royal Air Force then purchased Phantoms as did Japan, Korea, Turkey, Greece,

Left: Another Phantom, the II, takes to the air with its older brothers, the Demon and the Banshee. The F4H (F-4) Phantom II became one of the most successful fighters ever built. *MCAIR*

Iran, Israel, Spain, Germany and even Egypt. The Phantom was the principal air-to-air fighter in Vietnam for both the USAF and USN. On 24 May 1978, the 5,000th Phantom II was delivered, heralding a sales record that has been unequalled by any Century-series fighter.

In April 1967 when McDonnell Aircraft merged with Douglas Aircraft to form the McDonnell Douglas Aircraft Corporation, McDonnell was in the throes of being the US prime contractor for the exploration of space by producing both the Mercury and Gemini series of spacecraft. The growth and success of McDonnell Douglas since that time has been heralded by business experts.

The Company has a flavour all its own. Ever since the beginning, McDonnell believed in putting everything onto paper – memos, procedures, organisation, everything was written down. Today's procedures at McDonnell go back to these memos – a Control Procedures Manual came out of the memo books. McDonnell's forte was management. He realised if he was going to give the attention to detail that he wished, he would have to stop all other outside activity, and that included flying. If there was a lynchpin to the way that McDonnell ran his company it was loyalty. Rarely was he forced to fire anybody, and he was involved in everything, every part of the Company, even though he continued working beyond the mandatory retirement age of 70. Although the reins of the Company passed to Sanford 'Sandy' N. McDonnell, 'Mr Mac's' influence was keenly felt for many years. Every little detail was carefully scrutinised and looked at, no matter how small. This again is a carryover from 'Mr Mac's' personal style. *Business Week* magazine described it in this way, 'In few, if any companies its size, has a single man's influence been so pervasive.'

In style and tone, McDonnell Douglas directly mirrors 'Mr Mac's' personal characteristics. He built a company that is exceedingly inbred, paternalistic, dominated by engineers and infused with a penchant for penny-pinching. Company loyalty dictates and insiders get the important jobs. Rarely is anyone hired from the outside to do a major task. The Company doesn't have employees, it has 'teammates'.

In 1978 McDonnell Douglas was the Pentagon's leading prime contractor, as it had been for three years running. In 1977 it was awarded $2.6billion worth of orders compared with $1.7billion for the second-ranking Lockheed Corporation.

Looking back over his 80 years, before his death on 22 August 1980, Mac divided his life into two periods. The first 40 were of preparation, the last of fulfilment . . . right on schedule, right on plan to what he intended when he first started working as an aeronautical engineer. Out of this matrix came the F-15.

2. Enter the Dogfighter

At the end of World War 2 the American fighter pilot reigned supreme in what was generally considered to be the finest fighter developed by the combatants, the North American P-51 Mustang. While not as manoeuvrable as some of its contemporaries such as the Spitfire, the Mustang was endowed with long range, high cruise speed, good fire power and then once in the target area, capability to manoeuvre with its opponents and emerge victorious. After World War 2 the close-in manoeuvring fighter-to-fighter dogfight was dropped from Air Force thinking. Instead a new generation of jet bomber interceptors began to enter the inventories of air forces around the world. Yet, by 1950 jets were fighting it out over Korea during hard manoeuvring battles.

The F-86 Sabre emerged from that conflict with a 7:1 kill-to-loss ratio over the MiG-15 (10:1 for all USAF aircraft vs North Korean MiGs). The irony of this centres on the fact that the F-86 was designed as an escort fighter/dive bomber in the mid-1940s, not a dogfighter. Its low wing loading enabled it to have much the same turning capability as the P-51, selected, however, to permit high altitude interception, not to enhance manoeuvrability in a close-in fight.

After the Korean War, with the advent of air-to-air missiles, the prediction was again made, that the dogfight was over. This had been said after World War 1, after World War 2 and it was being said again

Below: North American Rockwell's mockup for the FX looked very much like the later YF-16.

Above: One of McDonnell's earlier configurations for the FX – a 60,000lb variable sweep wing aircraft.

after Korea as guns were being replaced by missiles. The claim of the technology advocates was that the missile would do the manoeuvring, therefore all that was required was a launch platform. The opposite turned out to be true. The missile, by eliminating the straight diving or accelerating escape, created new pressure toward the manoeuvring fight, as was quickly proven in the Vietnam War. Nevertheless, it seems that if one is to take the trends of fighter development through the 1950s, 1960s and into the 1970s, there has been a persistent desire, almost a leap of faith, to believe missiles are capable of being developed which cannot be outmanoeuvred or countermeasured and which have true all-aspect launch envelopes. In other words, there was a belief that no matter where the missile was fired, the opposing fighter could not escape it – the missile, at that point would truly do the manoeuvring. If this were indeed the case, then in fact the era of the fighter and the manned military aircraft would end. All that would be needed for perfect air defence would be a missile launch platform which could be anything from a lumbering transport to a launch rail on the ground. This belief seemed to have been accepted by the aircraft builders although not, it should be noted, by the fighter pilots. Missiles took over – guns disappeared from aircraft. The F-8 Crusader, a guns-plus-heat seeking-missile interceptor, was replaced by the F-4 Phantom II, a missile-only fleet defence interceptor.

In the late 1950s and early 1960s most tactical aircraft were either interceptors or, at the other end of the spectrum, nuclear strike bombers. For instance, the F-105 Thunderchief was the first tactical aircraft designed around a bomb bay to carry nuclear weapons. Surprisingly it incorporated a gun, although the primary missions had nothing to do with dogfighting. Some of this had to do with money – to get a piece of the Strategic Air Command pie, Tactical Air Command (TAC) had to get into nuclear delivery.

In the late 1950s, the USAF conceived another tactical nuclear bomber, the F-111. This was converted – on paper – into the TFX tri-service multi-mission 'fighter' by Dr Harold Brown, then Director of Defense Research and Engineering (DDR&E). He managed to convince Secretary of Defense Robert McNamara that, just as in the case of the tri-service F-4, great savings could be achieved by an aircraft common to all services. Later, when the F-111 was pressed into combat, it was found to have very poor conventional weapons delivery capabilities because its design philosophy had been centred on delivering a single nuclear weapon which left it short of both thrust and wing area when it was called upon to carry a substantial load of 'iron' bombs. The F-111 with 48 Mk 82s can't fly higher than 16,000ft.

To say that fighter pilots in all services in the United States found the 'no dog fight' philosophy uncomfortable would be an understatement. There were hard core groups of combat pilots who had experienced the reality of the manoeuvring dogfight – they would not give the concept up, realising that conventional wars would continue to be fought regardless of how much emphasis was placed on nuclear strike.

The Air Force, on the other hand, wanted to press forward with the F-105 and the F-111 due to Strategic Air Command dominance. Secretary McNamara saw a need for multi-mission conventional delivery aircraft so he forced the USAF to buy the F-4 starting with the F-4C (almost a copy of the USN F-4B), then allowed the Air Force to have its own versions in the F-4D and E.

As Brown made the F-111 into the TFX (Tactical Fighter Experimental) there was no real change from the nuclear role. The USAF became quite embarrassed with the F-111 disaster but continued to buy.

In 1964 and 1965 mumbles became louder from TAC to consider an air-to-air fighter while Brown and USAF Research & Development (R&D) experts began research on a US/West German V/STOL aircraft, a failure that later died. In the same time frame, an FX (Fighter Experimental) Study was initiated by Russ Murray, on behalf of McNamara's 'Whiz Kids', and Secretary of the Air Force Brown – it was a pure ton-mile bombing study comparing the A-7 to the F-5 done with USN behind-the-scenes support to force the Air Force to buy the A-7.

The A-7 was procured for the Air Force but USAF R&D decided a new fighter programme was needed to make up for the F-111. New concept studies under the name FX, regardless of confusion with the earlier studies, were started.

The new Commander of TAC, Gen Gabriel P. Disosway, was firmly behind a new fighter. FX studies were started by Tac Air (the tactical operations group), R&D section of the air staff, and a concept formulation phase started in December 1965 when the Air Force requested parametric studies. As a result, Air Force Systems Command (AFSC) came out with an 'optimum' solution: a 60,000lb variable sweep multi-purpose aircraft. That it looked so much like the F-111 shocked many people into reconsidering what was going on. By March 1966 industry was brought in to refine the 60,000lb 'fighter' with initial design studies contracted to North American Rockwell, Lockheed Aircraft and Boeing.

In October 1966 Maj John Boyd was assigned to the Pentagon to review the FX studies. Outspoken and aggressive, Boyd had been the most influential air-to-air tactician at the USAF Fighter Weapons School during the 1950s. In 1958 he had written a pioneering tactics manual entitled *Aerial Attack Study* which, for the first time, developed the logic of manoeuvre-countermanoeuvre sequences in aerial fighting, and emphasised the new concepts of vertical, out-of-plane, and three dimensional manoeuvring – all essential to the successful employment of the newer, less manoeuvrable Century-series fighters.

Not content with having revolutionised the qualitative logic of manoeuvring tactics in air combat, Boyd went on to develop a new quantitative theory for measuring and comparing the manoeuvring performance of opposing fighters . . . an energy approach to manoeuvring. Boyd found himself explaining it to a group of students at Georgia Tech in 1962 by referring to losing energy during hard turns in a dogfight. Boyd has since said, 'What happens is that in a hard turn your drag exceeds your thrust and at that point you have a negative energy rate. So when you have a negative energy rate, you have to lose altitude or airspeed or a combination thereof. To get energy rate, you multiply thrust minus drag times your velocity and it tells you how fast you're gaining or losing energy. It will come out in the form of gains or losses in altitude, airspeed, or both.'

After explaining this, Boyd realised he had come upon something new . . . something so simple that surely someone else would have thought about it. After graduating from Georgia Tech he was transferred to Eglin AFB, Florida, where he began attempting to go over his theories with some of his former associates. There was no interest until he came across Tom Christie, a mathematician who worked with computers at Eglin and who then gave Boyd access to a large amount of computer time.

In 1964 Boyd and Christie published their paper on energy manoeuvrability, bringing Boyd to the attention of senior officers in the Air Staff. They invited him to redo the trade-off studies on the FX to see if he could better the 60,000lb aircraft the Air Force Systems Command had produced.

The result, based on Boyd's theory, was the ideal of having a reasonably-sized fighter that could both out-accelerate and out-turn the enemy at all speeds encountered during a dogfight. To achieve this, thrust to weight ratio was extremely important as well as plenty of wing area relative to weight. Boyd's emphasis on air-to-air performace was instrumental in convincing the Air Staff to proceed with the FX as a single purpose air-to-air fighter, as opposed to the then-sacred multi-mission aircraft.

At the time, even with misgivings about the F-111's sluggish performace, the swing wing was regarded as the miracle wave of the future, and it seemed that everyone was thinking in these terms, including Boyd. As almost an afterthought he wondered what the trade-offs would look like for fixed wing . . . he began to think about the aerodynamic benefits versus the structural penalties in a variable sweep wing.

As it turned out Boyd started a whole new investigation into fixed wing versus swing wing. All the contractors except Northrop were in favour of the swing wing, but what began to emerge was a structural penalty for swing wings much larger than generally admitted, increasing as the fighter manoeuvrability requirements increased. This fell out as one of the answers to Boyd's questions. Of even more importance, the studies were the first since World War 1 in which a fighter had been designed to manoeuvre rather than to go higher and faster. Low wing loading or large wing area per weight after World War 2 seemed to be a result of the desire for high altitude flight. Now a fighter was being designed from inception to engage in dogfights.

The other end of the story, of course, was the engine. Boyd was making engine trade-offs with what designers call a 'rubber engine'. In other words engine size, temperature, pressure ratio and bypass ratio can be changed by computer at will to see how fighter performance improves or suffers. At the time Boyd entered the picture, the AFSC 'optimum' engine came out with a bypass ratio of approximately 2.2. This reflected the fashionableness of the turbofan or bypass engine, which pumps a great deal of cold air out of the first compressor stages without heating it in the combustion chamber. In other words, it is passed out around the side of the engine. High bypass engines are seen on most airliners today because they are very economical on fuel for long range flying. However, the problem with high bypass engines for fighters comes from their heavier weight and an afterburner which consumes more than the usual turbojet afterburner. Not mentioned at the time was the still unsolved tendency of afterburning fan engines to suffer severe stall/stagnation and overheating problems, particularly when manoeuvring.

The three basic sources for these studies were General Electric, Pratt & Whitney Aircraft and the Aeronautical Propulsion Laboratory at Wright Field. When Boyd raised the point that for the fighter mission a more efficient afterburner for combat would be needed rather than longer cruise range, and that 0.9 bypass ratio would be a lot better than 2.2, he created all kinds of thorns for the corporate problem solvers. A compromise was reached which came to 1.5 as a bypass ratio. Although Boyd really didn't think this was the proper solution, he later noted, 'you gotta give the bureaucracy time to adapt.'

Later studies under Boyd's tutelage revealed that a bypass ratio of 0.6 was even better than 0.9 but only marginally better than a bypass of 0; that is, a turbojet. At this point, in late 1967, DDR&E came up with the ill-conceived idea of forcing the new Navy and Air Force engines to share a common compressor/turbine core. This permitted no further engine optimisation and, in fact, forced the bypass ratio back up to over 0.7, together with equally unfavourable increases in temperature, compression ratio, weight and cost.

The FX itself remained a 60,000lb airplane for some time, but as the studies progressed and the requirements became more reasonable, by the spring of 1967 a more manoeuvrable 40,000lb fighter emerged, even though Boyd and his contemporaries considered this still too large. In July 1967 the Soviets held the Domodedovo Air Show near Moscow and presented the new high altitude Mach 2.9 MiG-25 'Foxbat' interceptor. It became a principal rationale for the FX, even though it proved to be incapable of dogfighting at normal tactical altitudes.

In August a request for proposal (RFP) was made to industry for a second concept formulation on the 40,000lb manoeuvrable FX. Another fighter theorist had entered the picture by this time, Pierre Sprey, working out of the Office of the Assistant Secretary of Defense for Systems Analysis. After being briefed by Boyd on his studies and his energy manouevrability theory, they got their heads together and began to think about how the FX could be improved even though by this time in late 1967 most of the FX designs were pretty solid.

These two men formed the nucleus of what has been labelled unofficially as 'the fighter mafia'. They laid out a smaller much hotter, less expensive aircraft in the 33-35,000lb class. The concept was presented to the Commander of the Air Force Systems Command who was sympathetic but unwilling to force the AFSC bureaucracy to go along. This rejection was to result in Sprey's FX^2 studies.

In an attempt to crystalise his logic on the value of a smaller, lightweight FX, Sprey noted in his 1969 OSO(SA) Staff Study on the FX^2: 'Because of the intense USAF pressure to hold a 40,000lb gross weight without relaxing the weight producing equipment/range/structural specifications, contractors are being forced into very expensive structural techniques with 45-50% titanium or other exotic materials. The FX^2 represents a large step increase in manoeuvring performance over the F-14 and F-15, with both 40% better maximum turn and 60% to 90% better acceleration. It has a large margin of transonic and supersonic sustained turn superiority. It achieves this remarkable increase by rigorously eliminating all weight-producing features of the aircraft not directly related to air-to-air capabilities while maximising all aircraft characteristics associated with air combat effectiveness. The aircraft is less than one-third as expensive as the F-14/F-15.'

This design was their last effort at trying to make the FX more austere although it later bore fruit by leading to the F-16. This extreme emphasis on air-to-air manoeuvring was of great value in overriding both Navy and OSD (DDR&E) commonality advocates who argued that the multi-mission Navy VFAX/F-14 would meet Air Force needs, and therefore, would lead to major savings (an echo of Harold Brown's arguments for the F-111/TFX). The Navy had never intended to produce the F-111B, cancelling it at the first favourable moment they could transfer the money to the Navy/Grumman designed F-14.

By December 1967 a six-month concept formulation study was underway at McDonnell Douglas and General Dynamics for the FX. In March 1968 competitive radar awards went to Hughes and Westinghouse. By September 1968 an RFP was released to industry for contract definition and the FX was then designated the F-15 as a replacement, not a stablemate, for the F-4E.

When the Development Concept Paper was approved, there were four areas that defined and justified the F-15. (1) single-seat, fixed wing, twin engine, approximately 40,000lb. (2) no competitive fly-off, deemed not suitable. (3) the VFX not a suitable F-4E replacement; nor could F-4E be modified to meet the threat. (4) air-to-ground capability, a fallout of the air-to-air mission.

Even though Sprey and Boyd were not able to make the F-15 significantly more austere, in 1969 the avionics and ground attack provisions were reduced slightly, reportedly lowering the unit cost by a claimed $1million. This anti-'goldplating' move was designed for cosmetic purposes so that the programme would not exceed $1billion, requiring Congressional approval. The originally planned radar set was modified and the TISEO (a complex telescopic TV camera) was eliminated due to cost.

The original F-15 programme had been laid out under the USAF/McNamara Total Package Procurement concept which involved massive paper studies, maximum documentation, no hardware competition and a single 'lock-in' contract covering development, testing, tooling and production.

Congressional and public criticism aroused by the C-5 and the F-111 cost overruns were making the F-15 SPO (Systems Program Office) at Wright-Patterson AFB very sensitive. As a result the Air Force slightly modified the F-15 Total Package Procurement to hold the contractor to demonstration milestones prior to obtaining additional funding.

The DCP was a step forward in preventing inflated estimates of performace with deflated costs and risks, the natural tendency in weapons procurement to get a product sold. The author has included the F-15 DCP in Appendix 5 verbatim with the exception of classified sections or extended discussions that did not bear inclusion – it is a fascinating first hand look into the inner workings of how a modern aircraft is developed.

When the F-15 contract was signed in December 1969, six areas in particular stood out: a) cost plus incentive fee in development; b) fixed price plus incentive fee in production; c) total system programme responsibility clause; d) limit of government obligation clause; e) forward pricing agreement; f) milestones to be met by the contractor before continuation of the programme.

The F-15 Demonstration Milestone Chart was written as follows:

(1)	Preliminary design review	9/70
(2)	Radar contractor selected	9/70
(3)	Critical design review	4/71
(4)	Avionics review	6/71
(5)	Major subassembly tests	6/72
(6)	Engine inlet compatability	3/72
(7)	FIRST FLIGHT	7/72
(8)	Bench avionics complete	9/72
(9)	1st A/C perf. demonstration	9/72
(10)	1st airborne avionics perf.	12/72
(11)	Fatigue test one lifetime	1/73
(12)	Static test 2 critical con.	1/73
(13)	Armament ground test	6/73
(14)	One G flight envelope	8/73
(15)	Fatigue test 3 lifetimes	12/73
(16)	AF evaluation summary	12/73
(17)	Equipment qualified	3/74
(18)	CAT II A/C & equip in place	3/74
(19)	Training equip in place	10/74
(20)	Fatigue test 4 lifetimes	10/74
(21)	Ext stores flutter release	8/74
(22)	AGE equipment in place	10/74
(23)	CAT I flight tests complete	11/74
(24)	FIRST AIRCRAFT TO TAC	11/74

During Phase IB, the first six months of contract definition, McDonnell conducted 10,150 hours of wind tunnel tests on MCAIR Model 199 as the F-15 was known at the time in St Louis.

After 12 months of paper competition among proposals, McDonnell Aircraft Co (MCAIR) of the McDonnell Douglas Corp was announced as the F-15 prime contractor in December 1969 winning over Fairchild and North American Rockwell. The FX studies had consumed over 2.5million manhours and 37,500 pages of reading, more than had been put into previous types before a decision.

Prior to this, in the preliminary design stage, literally thousands of configurations of all types were studied with the aid of McDonnell's Computer Aided Design and Evaluation program (CADE). The Programme 'tested' a wide variety of theoretical

Above: A good look at MCAIR's differential manoeuvring simulator. A pilot, sitting in an advanced fighter cockpit, looks over at an F-18 (projected model) 'flown' by a pilot in another part of the building. Both pilots are in turn 'chasing' a MiG. *MCAIR*

aircraft designs, including fixed and variable geometry, podded and fuselage mounted engines, single and two place cockpits, single and twin engine aircraft. The CADE-optimised aircraft however, turned out to have an aerodynamically inefficient 'rhomboid' wing which had to be redesigned with old-fashioned designer's judgement.

At MCAIR the F-15 really began with George Graff who headed up the design staff. Bob Little, former chief test pilot and engineer, was also inserted into the programme by his own request, but Graff controlled the design decisions while Don Malvern served as aerodynamist and programme manager for the aircraft.

Over 900 hours of air-to-air combat time in MCAIR's two cockpit air combat simulators in St Louis, pitting the MCAIR 199 against all postulated threats, had been spent to see if simulators could be used to improve the effectiveness of the design. Fighter pilots were finally having a say in what their aircraft could do and how the cockpits would be laid out; but the design variations had much less impact on combat outcome than the differences among the pilots flying the simulator. Some of the more experienced pilots concluded that the simulator taught tactics and habits that would prove fatal in combat.

The key to the F-15's current superior performance in manoeuvrability lies in the large wing area relative to weight. The wing has a low 65lb/sqft at clean take-off gross weight. During the wind tunnel test programme over 100 wing variations were tested at high angles of attack, at transonic and supersonic speeds. As many as 12 models at once were having air blown over them at various tunnels around the country. By the time the contract was awarded on 23 December 1969, five times the wind tunnel data as on the F-4 had been gathered for proposal submittal and paper evaluation, not on actual hardware.

The FX studies made by the Air Force and the Pentagon had brought about a fresh look into high angle of attack aerodynamics. Most wind tunnel testing previously had stopped at 12-14 degrees. The most critical wing design decision centred around using a highly cambered wing with no leading edge devices. This decision is still controversial, with critics claiming that the F-15 could have had significantly better lift at high angles of attack and reduced excessive supersonic drag with a flatter wing plus

Left: This is what an F-15 looked like after an engine bay fire. The titanium bay construction prevented fire from reaching the other engine – this survivability plus came out of research into F-4 losses in South-East Asia. *MCAIR*

Below: Launching of an AIM-7F Sparrow during tests early in the programme. *Raytheon via Stevenson*

movable leading edge. Many lessons were also drawn from the F-4 which had now seen quite a bit of combat experience. What enhanced survivability in combat? Why were so many F-4s lost due to hits in one engine knocking out both? What structures were most critical? Why were such a high percentage of F-4s lost due to fires?

The F-15's design resulted in a titanium keel to protect one engine bay from being destroyed by catastrophic failure of the other engine. Fire extinguishing systems were put in; titanium blankets surrounded the engines in an attempt to reduce fires and explosions, while no fuel tanks were located above or below the engines.

One interesting sidelight had nothing to do with the aerodynamics of the F-15 . . . McDonnell had a tough time naming the aircraft. With 'Mr Mac's' penchant for the supernatural, all kinds of long names were put in which did not sound as if they were aggressive or fighter-like. Two to three major efforts within the company to name the aircraft failed. Even contests to name the airplane didn't work.

When birds were considered, 'Mr Mac' was very specific about the limits. He was willing only to consider certain birds, frustrating everybody to death; yet there seemed to be no single person who had a brilliant idea. When the term Eagle came up it was immediately countered with the B-1 being up for that name, so they were going to have to be quick about it. 'Mr Mac' was willing to consider the name and once people began to get out their wildlife dictionaries and study the bird, it was found to be a fowl that hunts in bad weather. Considering the radar capabilities that were being built into the airplane and the desire to make it an all-weather aircraft, the name stuck.

In an Air Force that normally refers to its aircraft by number, the name Eagle seems to have caught on, even down to pilots wearing a patch entitled 'Eagle Driver'.

When the engine development studies were completed in September 1968, the race was on between General Electric and Pratt & Whitney to come up with the power plant that would give the F-15 a major increase in thrust to weight ratio. DDR&E forced the Navy and the Air Force to end up with a Joint Engine Program Office (JEPO) so a common engine core could power both the FX/F-15 and the F-14.

The B version of the F-14 was intended to use the F401 version of the common core engine, with only a different afterburner, fan and low stage compressor, while most other parts would be the same.

The Air Force was given primary responsibility by the Director of Defense Research and Engineering to develop the engine in April 1968.

In May 1968 RFPs were released to the industry for the initial engineering development on the FX engine. The Navy was asking for 27,000lb of thrust, while the Air Force wanted 22,000lb.

By March 1970 Pratt & Whitney was awarded the contract for the F100 engine, also to be developed under the milestone concept. Continuing the modified Total Package Procurement approach used for the airframe, there were eight milestones on the engine and each milestone was supposed to be met before further funding was available. The two most significant were standard features from previous engine programmes: the preliminary flight rating tests (PFRT) to be met by 31 March 1972 and the qualification test (QT) set for one year later. The Air Force approved full scale development funding by May 1973, after a few requirements were waived by Col Benjamin N. Bellis, head of the SPO at Wright Field.

The germinating fighter was also to carry two weapons, the GAU-7 25mm cannon and the AIM-82 infra-red missile, in addition to the new AIM-7F version of the radar guided Sparrow missile. Concern was voiced over the weight and complexity that would be added as a result.

The first demonstration milestone for the aircraft was coming up by September 1970 when the preliminary design review would be held. In the meantime, weapons and avionics were consuming a great deal of time. Computer studies were being run at furious paces, particularly in regards to the kill capability of the aircraft with its new weapons.

The 'Tac Avenger' computer programme study equipped the F-15 with the AIM-7F Sparrow and a gun versus the MiG-21 with the AIM-7F and a gun. The study revealed that the F-15 should have a kill to loss ratio of 18:1. Fighter pilots considered this a bit optimistic. Then the F-15 was mounted with the AIM-82 with a 50° off bore sight capability, while the MiG-21 was equipped with the AIM-7F and a gun. Incredibly, the USAF Studies and Analysis office at Headquarters Air Force came up with a kill to loss ratio of 955:1 in favour of the Eagle. When the findings were released in the form of a chart and a report, the fighter pilots had a hard time believing that these people were serious.

A high ranking general was briefed on the study and he said that if he believed it, which he didn't, then all the Air Force would need was one F-15 in the Far East, one in Europe and one in the States to train in. In short order the chart was shamefacedly withdrawn, but it is significant to note that the Air Force was still placing a great deal of faith in miracle weapons such as an all-aspect missile. The Sparrow, even in its latest form (the E-2) had not demonstrated a kill probability better than 10.6% in Linebacker I and II.

The new gun for the F-15, the 25mm GAU-7 cannon, was to be selected from a competition between Philco Ford and General Electric. What made the system unique was a caseless form of ammunition which had failed in 15 years of Army development. In December of 1971 there was a 'shoot off' between the competitors and Philco Ford was awarded the contract.

The uniqueness of the GAU-7 was incapsulated rounds . . . in other words, no hard case to contain the powder. Problems came up right away in that it was

Right: Installation mock up on the F-15 for the General Electric GAU-7 25mm cannon. Based on caseless ammunition, the weapon had problems that could not be solved. The M61 20mm Vulcan was installed in its place. *MCAIR*

BORESIGHT/FWD
GUN MOUNT ACCESS
MANUAL GUN
ROTATION
FS
429.75
FS
466.37
OPERATIVE

Above: The F-15 mock up at MCAIR. Though the basic shape is there, a number of refinements were made, including the elimination of the ventral fins resulting in greater vertical fin area. *USAF*

necessary to protect the ammunition itself from fire and weather. This necessitated an insulated lining in the aircraft structure around the ammunition compartment, tunnel and a portion of the gun bay. In addition, an intumescent paint coating was to be provided in the ammunition tunnel to help protect against high energy projectiles cooking off. Sufficient ventilation area was to be provided to preclude over pressure of the aircraft structure in the event of an ammunition burn.

Another problem was inconsistent ballistic action times. The ammunition was simply not reliable. As far back as the fall of 1969 the Air Force had defined the 20mm M61 gun as the initial system for the F-15 'until such time as a firm government decision can be made that a 25mm gun system is acceptable for aircraft installation', however the Air Force continued to require that all design criteria for the aircraft would fit the 25mm system.

By the end of September 1973 it became apparent that the gun design had not progressed to the point of installation, despite the expenditure of over $100million in development. The major problems were identified as follows: a nonworkable encapsulated feed system; a gun which cannot fire reliably at the high firing rate of 6,000rpm; incompatibility with blast deflection devices; and most of all, an unreliable and nonrepeatable round of ammunition of very limited environmental capability. In other words, it would burn and explode easily.

Philco Ford proposed a 12-month delay, but the programme was cancelled. The AIM-82 was also cancelled, although well before any commitment to hardware. The main reasons for cancellation were the extravagant requirements established by AFSC and the 955:1 claims. The criticism focused on the Air Force placing a great deal of faith in unproved technology that offered no real advantage over existing weapons. At the time Everest Riccioni, another one of the fighter mafia, predicted that in 1990 the primary weapon systems in the F-15 would still be the short range AIM-9 Sidewinder and the 1954 M61 20mm cannon. So far he has not been proven wrong.

By 1 July 1970 a fly-off radar competition had commenced at St Louis between Westinghouse and Hughes. By 31 August the radar fly-off was completed, the award going to Hughes. The first demonstration milestone, the preliminary design review, was completed in September 1970. The next month Hughes was selected to develop and build the attack radar.

By January 1971 there was an engine mock-up review and when the preliminary mock-up was ready on the F-15, the reaction of the fighter mafia when they came in to look at it was astonishment. John Boyd walked in the door, saw it and said, 'Good grief! It's too big!' but the trend had been set. The top plan form size on the Eagle came to 1,050sq ft as compared to 750sq ft for the F-4 and 375sq ft for the F-5.

Things were progressing very well in spite of a few setbacks, primarily related to the engine (see Chapter

5). In February 1971 the surveys and investigation staff of the House Appropriations Committee had completed a comparative study of the F-14 and F-15 including that both aircraft were equally manoeuvrable, but that the F-14 could accomplish the missions of both while the F-15 could not. This quickly brought out the critics of the Department of Defense as well as those who had continued to say that a common aircraft should be developed for both services rather than one for each. The Air Force came back quickly saying that the F-14 had been developed for fleet air defence as a missile interceptor while the F-15 was strictly a manoevring offensive fighter that could be made suitable for aircraft carrier operation, but did not possess the extremely sophisticated Phoenix missile system. Since the Eagle was designed for supreme manoeuvrability, it was quickly pointed out that past experience, as seen in the F-111 and other aircraft, resulted in a lack of manoeuvrability when aircraft were developed for common use in both services.

As the 3rd and 4th milestones were completed in April and May 1971, in the form of a critical design review and an avionics equipment development review, both the F-14 and the F-15 were still coming under fire from Congress, particularly from the Peace Through Law members who numbered more than 100. Their *Report on the F-14 and F-15 Tactical Fighters* recommended funding for the development of a light, highly manoeuvrable FX^2 type fighter that

Below: 13 May 1972 – The first F-15 Eagle, MCAIR F-1, stands with F-4s just before being finished for roll out.

Above: Roll out of the first F-15, May 1972. *MCAIR*

could be produced at a cost significantly below that of the F-14 and could be used in combination with or as a substitute for the F-15. The proposal was defeated and both aircraft went on, but it was obvious that the lightweight fighter was beginning to see its day.

In July 1971 the SPO was approached by the Secretary of Defense with a request to investigate development of an F-15N, an Eagle for the Navy. MCAIR responded that with a minimum of modifications, the aircraft could be made suitable for carrier use, but the Navy pushed on with their own study, increasing the weight and putting Phoenix missiles onboard. The weight and drag increased to such a point that performance was drastically reduced and the cost went out of sight. Many thought the matter closed, but in March 1973 another investigation was made by the Senate Armed Services Committee to discuss modifying the F-15 for the Navy, since the F-14 was still having severe problems. Deputy Secretary of Defense Clements favoured an Air Force versus Navy fly-off battle, with F-15N vs F-14D test costs in July 1973 estimated by the reluctant services at $150,000,000 for the FY 1974 budget. This was to result in the F-15 as an alternative for the Navy-Marine Corps fighter modernisation programme. There were some heated discussions about flying the two aircraft off against each other, one pilot belligerently insisting that live ammunition be placed in both aircraft to make the solution final.

By February 1972 the prototype F100 engine had completed 60 hours of testing and milestone five, structural test of major aircraft subassemblies, was completed a good three months ahead of schedule. The first test radar was also delivered to MCAIR and milestone six, engine inlet compatability tests, was completed.

The programme was facing few serious problems. On 26 June 1972 the first F-15, designated MCAIR F-1, was rolled out at St Louis to the pride of everyone who had taken part. In July the aircraft was airlifted to Edwards AFB, California in a C-5A.

3.
The Eagle Flies

On 27 July 1972, McDonnell chief test pilot Irv Burrows lifted the first F-15A, Air Force serial number 71-280, into the air. After the flight he made the comment, 'It was just like the simulator!'

McDonnell had the benefit of developing one of the finest flight simulators in existence. Long before the first flight the aircraft had been 'flown' numerous times by McDonnell's test pilots, not only in normal flight regimes, but in air-to-air dogfights. The simulator, which is still in extensive use in the F-18 programme and follow-on programme for development of the F-15, consists of 40ft spherical chambers with cockpits mounted on the floor. The device gives a projection of air-space and one or two other aircraft, enabling simulation of one-on-one or two-on-one combat. This is far from the many-on-many situation typical of real combat, but it allows some wringing out of the aircraft. Once one is plugged into the simulator, complete with oxygen mask, realistic cockpit displays and controls, and the dynamic parameters to approximate the aircraft one is flying, the action becomes quite realistic inside the cockpit. The exterior view, however, leaves a bit to be desired. After all, the opposing aircraft that one sees from the cockpit are only TV projected models on the walls of the chamber. Afterburners light, missiles come off rails, missile hits are observed and one can see the earth turning around the cockpit. The pilots hear flight noises and the sound of their own missile and gunfire. As they fly through tight turns, their bodies feel pressure through hooked up G-suits although the actual G-forces cannot be duplicated. This three-aircraft dogfight requires a computer which executes up to 2,500,000 instructions per second to keep the action going.

Twenty pre-production F-15's were designated for the test programme. Twelve for contractor development and eight for Air Force evaluation. The

Below: MCAIR test pilot Irv Burrows rotates for lift-off, Edwards AFB, CA, for the Eagle's first flight, 27 July 1972. *USAF*

prototypes and their missions were designated from F-1 and TF-1 as follows:

F-1: open the F-15 flight envelope and explore handling qualities; external stores. First flight 27 July 1972.
F-2: the prime engine test airframe. First flight 26 September 1972.
F-3: avionics test bed, first aircraft with APG-63 radar, calibrated air-speed tests. First flight 4 November 1972.
F-4: structural tests. First flight 13 January 1973.
F-5: first aircraft to have GE M61 20mm cannon, armament testing, jettison of external fuel. First flight 7 March 1973.
F-6: second avionics test bed; flight control evaluations; missile fire control. First flight 23 May 1973.
F-7: armament tests and fuel stores. First flight 14 June 1973.
TF-1: first two seater evaluation. First flight 7 July 1973.
F-8: spin recovery tail chute, high angle of attack work; fuel system. First flight 25 August 1973.
F-9: aircraft/engine performance. First flight 20 October 1973.
F-10: evaluation of Tactical Electronic Warfare System; radar; avionics. First flight 16 January 1974.

Below: During the F-15's first flight, Burrows has gear and flaps down as the chase plane flies formation. *USAF*

Bottom: A fine study of the first Eagle, with EROS Collision Avoidance Equipment mounted, at Edwards AFB.

Above: MCAIR F-3 served as the avionics test bed and it was the first Eagle with the APG-63 radar installed – first flight was made on 4 November 1972. *USAF*

Left: MCAIR F-6 making its first flight on 23 May 1973 – note the notched stabilators but the old unraked wingtip and small speedbrake. *MCAIR*

Below left: TF-1, the first two-seater, airborne on 12 July 1973 just five days after its first flight. *MCAIR*

Between F-7 and F-8 the first TF-15 was built, a two-seater. From that point on every seventh aircraft has been coming off the McDonnell Douglas line as a TF, now designated F-15B and F-15D depending on internal fuel capacity.

Divided into three categories, the test programme was made up of an Air Force Joint Test Force (JTF) with Tactical Air Command fighter pilots and Air Force Systems Command test pilots, as well as McDonnell Douglas test pilots. McDonnell Aircraft was to conduct Category I which is now called Contractor Development, Test and Evaluation, Category II, now called Air Force Development, Test, and Evaluation, and Category III, now Follow-On Operational Test and Evaluation, was handled by the Air Force.

F-1 to F-10 and the first two TFs were placed into Category I, while Category II included the last eight single-seat F-15s. As things turned out some of the Category I aircraft were transferred to the Air Force when MCAIR had completed their programme.

As the flight test programme got underway, there were remarkably few problems, with some exceptions. A stick-force gradient of 3.7lb per 'g' pulled resulted in as much as 25lb of steady pressure during long periods of manoeuvring at high 'g'. A second lower stick-force gradient was added to the system that comes into effect during high 'g'. There was also superfluous ramp change on the variable geometry inlets. The computer gains were reduced to make the system less responsive.

The pilots found cross-wind landings tricky at first due to the aircraft's low wing loading and narrow landing gear. The up-wind wing tended to come up and the aircraft wanted to weather vane into the wind while drifting downwind. The problem was aggravated by the Control Augmentation System (CAS) which includes a rudder-aileron interconnect to reduce adverse yaw, with a desensitised roll control feature when the stick is aft to minimise the F-15's tendency to depart and spin when rolled at high angles of attack. The net result from the pilot's view was that moving the stick into the cross-wind position did little to level the wings, yet aggravated the weather-vane tendency. The fix was a relatively easy one. MCAIR eliminated the rudder-aileron interconnect at touchdown when wheel spin indicated high speeds and the aileron control washout was eliminated with the gear down.

Left: F-1 on 26 September 1973 with three external fuel tanks hung – note the orange day-glo paint on the wings and vertical tail surfaces. *MCAIR*

The many hours spent in wind tunnel testing began to pay off. Only four months after flight testing began, the engine inlet compatability was finalised in the F-15. By comparison, the F-4 took 22 months and the F-101 took 30 months.

Initial pilot reaction to the Eagle was very favourable. The pilots found they had an aircraft that was not only quite manoeuvrable and powerful, having a thrust to weight ratio greater than 1:1, but a fighter that was very easy to fly. The Control Augmentation System provides more extensive 'artificial' stability corrections than previous flight controls. It senses pitch, roll and yaw rates, vertical and lateral acceleration, speed, angle of attack, stick and rudder inputs and then based on these, calculates appropriate commands to actuate each of the control surfaces. This basically interposes a computer between the pilot and the control surfaces, reducing the possibility of getting the airplane into a manoeuvring region where dangerous departures or spins may occur . . . but at the cost of some restriction in pilot stick and rudder options and heavy reduction in roll response at high 'g'. The computer does make the airplane safer and more predictable.

By the fall of 1974 only 36 ECPs (Engineering Change Proposals) had been recommended, 23 involving the aircraft, which were incorporated in the first and second production aircraft. Three of the problems resulted in external configuration changes.

The stabilator was found to flutter so the designers put a snag or notch in the leading edge creating a minor shift in the coefficient of pressure. A change in moment of inertia resulted. By the fourth F-15 the notch, on production aircraft, was retrofitted to the first three pre-production aircraft.

There was also a buffet problem in a small but very critical part of the envelope – around 30,000ft and Mach 0.85 to Mach 0.95 while pulling 6g or more. The problem was so bad that the pilots were afraid that the aircraft would break apart. The instruments were shuddering so badly they couldn't be read. The cause was an excessive airload on the wing beyond that predicted.

Engineering went to work. The wingtips were raked and cut back so that three square feet of area per side was removed. This was done on F-4 in March 1974 so that no production aircraft had the old tip. The problem was caused by the back part of the wing getting an inordinate amount of lift in this portion of the envelope.

The third major external change involved the speed brake which produced buffeting. MCAIR

Left: F-2 on 15 January 1973 without tail, wingtip and speedbrake modifications. *USAF*

Below: NASA's Dryden Flight Research Center, located at Edwards AFB, took on two F-15s (this is F-2) to evaluate data for future designs. The aim of the programme was to determine the cause for discrepancies between predicted and actually measured aerodynamic drag. *NASA*

Right: June 1974 – An F-15A approaches a tanker near Edwards. Note that the wingtips have not been 'raked' yet while the stabilators have been notched. *USAF*

enlarged the brake from 20 to 31.5sq ft to produce the needed drag at lower extension angles.

The SPO planned on 690,000 production hours through the completion of the first five aircraft. The actual number of hours came to 466,000. By April 1974 32% fewer manhours were required for assembly of the F-15 than originally estimated. MCAIR was finding very little production line scrapage. Since the F-15 contract required performance milestones, McDonnell had a great deal at stake in turning the aircraft out with as little waste as possible. Six performance milestones had been required of MCAIR by the end of 1974. By April 1973, less than a year after the initial flight, and with prototype engines installed, four of six milestones had been exceeded. The full scale inlet with the F100 engine had also been mated to the aircraft at Arnold Engineering Development Center in Tullahoma, Tn. The problems involved, which were rather extensive on previous aircraft involving supersonic flight, hopefully had been solved in the wind tunnel.

The SPO had also ordered, as was standard procedure, a full-scale mock up of the flight control system so that pilots could establish positioning for the controls and instruments before anything was actually built. To save cost, Litton Systems inertial platform specifications were eased to a three nautical mile error, and unexpectedly the system had less than one nautical mile error.

Regardless of the efforts by the SPO and MCAIR to cut costs, overruns began to mount as problems were encountered. By December 1979, according to the official Selected Acquisition Report (see Appendix 3), the programme cost overrun had increased by several billion dollars.

Continually on the Air Force's back was the spectre of the F-14 and the trouble the Navy was having with that airplane. There was a great deal of inter-service rivalry involving the two aircraft. Design proposals were made on both sides of the fence, one being to modify the F-15 for Navy use, the other to modify the F-14 for Air Force use. Memos, fact sheets and all kinds of data were passing back and forth in the Pentagon and the Department of Defense trying to convince people of both sides.

The F100 engine became a major thorn in the flesh for Bellis and his team. There had been fuel control and afterburner problems. Those taking potshots delighted in pointing out that the engine had not flown until it had been installed in the F-15, therefore compounding the problem with two experimental units being tested simultaneously. The F-15 fit into

the small category of having three simultaneous development problems: new engines, new airframe and new avionics.

Sure enough the F100 began to act up in the first ten months of 1973. It broke down several times, fires resulted, even explosions. Those with faith in the engine and the aircraft were sure that the problems could be overcome, but the pressure was heavy. The engine endurance qualification test was the only milestone that the F-15 failed to meet on time. In February 1973, the engine failed a fan and a turbine blade before the 150-hour milestone that was to be reached the next May.

To meet the deadline, General Bellis relaxed the requirements of two parts of the engine endurance test, the very high Mach and high altitude portions, to allow the milestone to be reached on time. He was jumped on for trying to push something under the carpet and get the aircraft through its tests without any blemishes. The problem was related in part to rust inside the test chamber walls which had dislodged and coated the turbine blades, affecting their cooling and aerodynamic capabilities. However, a real endurance problem surfaced that has stayed with the engine, proving stubborn to a solution. The F100 engine was delivered on 12 October 1973 but the engine has had its share of problems, resulting in a number of fixes.

Some of the changes involved the idle setting at high altitude which had to be adjusted on the Series 1 YF100 pre-production version from a constant 60% rpm to 71-72% since so much throttle movement had been required to get up to military power – and fast throttle movement at high altitude frequently led to engine stalls.

The five-segment afterburner encountered transient pressure buildups between segments – again leading to stalls – early in the flight test programme while pilots were moving the throttle through the afterburner select range. This was ameliorated with modifications in the spray nozzles, fuel leads, and spray bars. Fuel pump problems forced several in-flight engine shutdowns and caused afterburner unlights or blowouts.

By the end of 1973 production manhours on the F-15 had come to 80% of that on the F-4, due to extensive use of large integrally machined parts, eliminating many of the joints normal to aircraft construction. Fabrication of parts consumes just over half of the total F-15 production manhours and two-thirds of those are in fabricating titanium, 26.5% of which makes up the F-15 versus 9% in the F-4. Some composites are used in the F-15 such as boron and graphite epoxies, incorporated in the horizontal stabilators and in the vertical tails. These are placed over titanium frames, spars and torque boxes, which are faced with boron epoxy skin over full depth aluminium honeycomb. The titanium bulkheads are machined down to 145lb from 1,250lb of metal. The centre section contains all four of the fuselage fuel tanks and, directly adjacent to the fuel, the engine inlets. The forward section contains the pilot and the avionics while the rear section contains the side-by-side engines in all-titanium bays, resulting in isolation of each engine from the other as was shown in the test programme when one engine blew up and failed to burn through the bulkheads to the other engine.

The more MCAIR and Air Force pilots who flew the F-15 at Edwards, the more everyone realised that the Air Force had finally returned to the manoeuvring performance needed in a close-in aerial combat fighter. The lessons of Vietnam and its poor kill ratios were fresh and pilots were exulting in the step forward of their new fighter.

The aircraft's most significant advance was its energy manoeuvrability, or its capability to turn, accelerate or climb in order to gain a tactical advantage. The large bubble canopy on top of the airplane which cost it a bit in aerodynamic efficiency nevertheless provided the much needed ability to look 360 degrees around the aircraft.

SYSTEM/INSTALLATION	F-15 	F-4E 
COCKPIT INSTRUMENTS	30	48
NUMBER OF AVIONIC "BLACK BOXES"	106	294
FLIGHT CONTROL DEVICES	9	16
NUMBER OF ELECTRICAL CONNECTORS	808 (SILICONE GROMMETS)	905 (POTTED)
FUEL SYSTEM PLUMBING CONNECTIONS	97	281
HYDRAULIC FILTERS	7	21
LUBRICATION POINTS (ALL SYSTEMS)	202	510
FASTENER TYPES	1200	2800
DRAG CHUTE REQUIRED	NO	YES

Above: F-15/F-4E component comparison.

Landing and take-off were found to be very simple procedures and the aircraft could be flared down to a touch-down speed of approximately 120kts.

The aircraft's Mach 2.5 capability, however, was found to be a misleading statistic. If an F-15 took off in full afterburner to make a high speed intercept, it could get no further than 70 nautical miles before having to return. In addition, the exotic materials required to go this fast – variable ramp inlets and special metals – add to the cost and the weight. The irony of this is that Mach 2.5 capability is not relevant tactically (see Chapter 7) and that with four Sparrow and four Sidewinder missiles, the F-15 cannot fly faster than Mach 1.78. Below 10,000ft the missiles and the drag of the conical camber wing creates a difference in top speed between the F-15 and the F-5 of less than 80 knots.

Because of the complexity of on-board systems, considerable attention was paid to maintenance convenience. The engines are interchangeable because the engine accessory drive unit is mounted on the airframe instead of on the inside of the engine. The F-15 has 570sq ft of access doors, 230sq ft of which is comprised of 67 non-structural quick-access doors with latches that require only a half turn with a screwdriver to open. This amounts to four times the area of quick access doors on the F-4E.

MCAIR was also guaranteeing 11.3 maintenance manhours per flight hour (MMH/FH) as opposed to what was then 24 on the F-4E. This was getting back down to the P-51, the lowest cost fighter as far as hours required in maintenance that the Air Force has ever had, although this low figure has never been reached in line units, where MMH/FH were up to 35 by 1980. This does not include the hours put in by contractor maintenance personnel. The F-15 can be turned around in 12 minutes for re-launching in an air-to-air configuration, 45% quicker than the F-4E. MCAIR was able to deliver the 21st F-15 off the line as the first production model, compared to the 48th F-4 being the first production model.

The F-15 is about one foot longer and four feet wider in span than the F-4E, but it weighs considerably less and has a much greater wing area, 608sq ft as compared to 503sq ft, which results in a combat loading (60% internal fuel remaining) of approximately 60lb/sq ft in combat (40% fuel burned off) compared to 80lb/sq ft for the F-4. The excess thrust (Ps) of the engines enables the aircraft to be muscled into firing position without the pilot having to resort to energy-building manoeuvres such as dives and zoom climbs, the problem faced in air-to-air combat previously.

Just over two years after the Eagle's first flight, Col Wendell Shawler, former director of the F-15 Joint Test Force, and then Vice Commander of the 495th Test Wing, and Irv Burrows, chief test pilot for McDonnell, took the second TF-15 to Farnborough, England for the International Air Show. On 26 August 1974, they took off from Loring AFB, Maine and flew non-stop to Bentwaters, England in 5.3 hours. The aircraft was equipped with additional fuel pallets attached to the side of the F-15 fuselage under the wings, called FAST (Fuel and Sensor Tactical) Packs, carrying an additional 10,000lb of fuel to nearly double the ferry range. Flying 92 demonstration flights in 43 days, the TF-15 averaged 4.25 MMH/FH.

By 30 September 1974 the Eagle had made its 3,000th flight and by 14 November the Category I and II R&D flight test programme was completed with the delivery of the first production F-15 (TF-3) to Tactical Air Command at Luke Air Force Base, Arizona. The Eagle went to the 555th Tactical Fighter Training Squadron, better known as the 'Triple Nickel', which scored 40 MiG victories over Vietnam. The 'Nickel' would now be responsible for training future Eagle pilots.

Above left: Two early block number Eagles, gear just coming up, at Edwards, in May 1974. *MCAIR*

Left: The first operational F-15, a TF, nicknamed TAC 1, was delivered to the 555th ('Triple Nickel') TFTS at Luke AFB on 14 November 1974. Here, from left to right, USAF Chief of Staff, Gen David Jones, 'Nickel' CO Lt-Col Ted Laudise and President Gerald Ford look over the two-seater. A Secret Service man stands to the far right. *USAF*

Below: TF-15 71-291 was the FAST Pack pallet prototype. The pallets produce quite a bit of extra room for fuel and equipment extending from inlets to tail. This aircraft flew to the Farnborough Air Show non-stop unrefuelled across the Atlantic from St Louis in September 1974. Note a MCAIR markings peculiarity that started with the F-4: the national insignia has no blue surround to the bars or the blue circle; yet the wing insignia is standard. This has become an unofficial MCAIR trademark. *MCAIR*

After 7,300 hours' flying time on 47 F-15s, the first F-15 was lost on 15 October 1975. This put the F-15 in the category of being the only fighter to achieve its first 5,000 flying hours without an accident.

Accident Rate Summary at 145,000 Hours

Aircraft	*Strikes*	
	No	*Rate*
F-4	20	13.8
F-14	20	14.5
F-5	15	10.3
F-111	14	9.7
F-15	10	6.9

By early 1975 the Air Force and MCAIR had their heads together on configuring a special Eagle to break a number of records that had previously been held by the F-4 and the MiG-25. Operation 'Streak Eagle' was activated with the 19th pre-production aircraft, F-17. Everything that could be stripped from the aircraft was removed, including the missiles, radar, cannon, tail hook, several actuators, one of the generators, the utility hydraulic system, even down to no paint on the airplane.

Between 16 January and 1 February 1975 this F-15 set eight altitude and time-to-climb records. Five records were established in one day on three flights, each flown by a different pilot out of Grand Forks AFB, North Dakota. Empty, the 'Streak Eagle'

World Class Time-to-climb Records
Time in seconds from brake release

Altitude	*Previous time*	*Held by*	*F-15 time*	*Pilot/Date*	*Margin*
3,000m (9,843ft)	34.52	F-4	27.57	Maj R. Smith 16 January 1975	20%
6,000m (19,685ft)	48.79	F-4	39.33	Maj W. R. Macfarlane 16 January 1975	19%
9,000m (29,528ft)	61.68	F-4	48.86	Maj W. R. Macfarlane 16 January 1975	21%
12,000m (39,370ft)	77.14	F-4	59.38	Maj W. R. Macfarlane 16 January 1975	23%
15,000m (49,212ft)	114.50	F-4	77.02	Maj D. W. Peterson 16 January 1975	33%
20,000m (65,617ft)	169.80	MiG-25	122.94	Maj R. Smith 19 January 1975	28%
25,000m (82,021ft)	192.60	MiG-25	161.02	Maj D. W. Peterson 26 January 1975	16%
30,000m (98,425ft)	243.86	MiG-25	207.80	Maj R. Smith 1 February 1975	15%

Far left: In January 1975 the F-15 broke several world class time-to-climb records flying from Grand Forks AFB, North Dakota, during Project 'Streak Eagle'. Here the cleaned up F-15A gets away on one of the runs. *MCAIR*

Top left: The F-15 'Streak Eagle'. Excess weight was eliminated even down to the paint. The aircraft accelerated so rapidly that some runs had to be aborted due to exceeding gear down speed before the landing gear could fully retract. *MCAIR*

Centre left: The 'Streak Eagle' making one of its runs from Grand Forks AFB, North Dakota. The aircraft was restrained until full power was reached, then released. In 400ft and 4.5sec after release it was airborne.

Below: Preparing for the time-to-climb flight to 30,000m on 2 February 1975. *Douglas Slowiak via Stevenson*

weighed 2,800lb less than the production aircraft dry. Depending on the flight requirements, only enough fuel was carried to fly each profile and return to the airfield. A hold back device was installed so that the aircraft could run up to full power and then release, go down the runway, rotate and lift off to make its run. Even in the standard F-15 a pilot cannot run up above 80% power and hold brakes or the aircraft will begin to drag itself across the ground.

The acceleration was so phenomenal that the pilots had to abort a few runs as they passed gear extension speed before the wheels retracted. The pilot couldn't go down the runway, rotate, then hit the gear handle fast enough to get the gear in the wells before the doors were stressed beyond their limits.

The 3,000m record flight was piloted by Maj Roger Smith. With a thrust to weight ratio at release at over 1.6 to 1 the 'Streak Eagle' lifted off the ground after a roll of only 400ft, approximately seven airplane lengths. Smith quickly raised the landing gear and maintained nearly level flight while accelerating to approximately Mach 0.6. The aircraft was then rotated by a 5g pullup to a near vertical climb attitude. The Eagle accelerated during this climb to Mach 1 and reached the specified 3,000m altitude (9,843ft) in 27.57sec. The 6,000m, 9,000m and 12,000m records were set by Maj Willard 'Mac' MacFarlane in one flight of 16 January. The profile was similar to the 3,000m flight except that a maximum speed of Mach 0.7 was obtained before the pullup. MacFarlane and his Eagle were at sonic speed only 23sec after release.

The third flight on 16 January was made by Maj Dave Peterson for the 15,000m record. On this and subsequent flights pilots were wearing pressure suits. Upon lift-off Maj Peterson accelerated about 50ft over the runway to 0.65 Mach and pulled into a 55° flight path angle to reach the 15,000m target altitude (49,212ft) in 77.05sec. This is approximately 10sec quicker to that altitude than the Saturn V rocket boosted the Apollo spacecraft on its way to the moon.

The 20,000m profile with Maj Smith again at the controls consisted of a giant Immelmann manoeuvre starting at Mach 0.65 on the deck and pulling 2.5g until the airplane was over the top at 32,000ft and accelerating in the opposite direction from take-off. While passing through 20,000ft the Eagle was vertical with a 2.5g load factor and a rate of climb faster than the speed of sound. At Mach 1.5 Smith pulled 4g into a 55° climb and held it there to 66,617ft in 122.94secs elapsed time. The margin over the 'Foxbat' record was 28%.

Maj Peterson then took over for the 25,000m record and flew a similar profile. Maximum speed achieved was Mach 1.8 just prior to the second pullup. The specified altitude of 82,021ft was achieved in 161.02sec at a speed of Mach 0.6. The aircraft eased over the top of the climb and descended without incident. This beat the 'Foxbat's' time by 17%.

In 1973 the MiG-25 climbed to 30,000m in 4min 3.86sec. When Maj Smith made the flight to break this record, he lifted off the runway at a weight of 32,000lb after 500ft of ground roll, accelerating to Mach 0.65 and then pulling into a 2.5g Immelmann similar to the two previous record profiles. After rolling 180° at the top of the climb Smith accelerated in a slight climb to build up total energy. The 'Streak Eagle' passed through Mach 2 approximately 21 miles down range and two minutes from take-off. At Mach 2.2 Smith pulled up to 4g and attained a 55° flight path whereupon the stick was relaxed to maintain a constant climb attitude. The 30,000m mark (98,425ft) was achieved in 207.08sec, bettering the 'Foxbat' time by 36sec. The aircraft maintained a nearly ballistic free fall path as it went over the top at 102,400ft.

Less than a year later, on 9 January 1976, the first F-15 landed at Langley AFB, Virginia to be delivered to the 1st Tactical Fighter Wing, a unit rich in history with squadrons that date back to World War 1.

At Langley the 1st Wing had to prepare the physical facilities required to build and operate an F-15 wing, organise a unit from a central five-man cadre, and initiate pilot and maintenance training to provide for adequate numbers of trained personnel to keep pace with the 1976 aircraft delivery schedule. As the Wing began to gear up, problems mounted. Even though the aircraft was a fighter pilot's dream, there were many unforeseen difficulties.

The first problems with the aircraft began to show up at the 555th Tactical Fighter Training Squadron and the 461st Tactical Fighter Training Squadron at Luke. They had the responsibility of taking new pilots out of Air Training Command as well as transitioning veteran pilots into the F-15. Sorties and flying hour goals became difficult to meet due to an extensive optimism concerning the maintainability and reliability of F-15 systems. Consequently operations in TAC started with an advertised capability of 1.13 sorties per aircraft per day. However, as things turned out, a 0.61 sortie production rate (SPR) was the best achieved, even then only with considerable difficulty according to those involved in the programme.

As Capt Tom Lennon and Capt Jim Wray, both pilots in the 1st Tac Fighter Wing, put it, 'There were a number of factors in the real world of blue suit operations that degraded the actual sortie production rate. Aircraft reliability in that first year measured by mean time between failures (MTBF) was less than one-half that predicted. It took considerably longer to repair each failure and spare parts did not cover the needs. Aircraft available to fly averaged just over one-half the initial expectation. And the SPR reflected these factors.'

Col Larry D. Welch, commander of the Wing, was determined to produce results regardless of the problems. This new air superiority fighter had to be exploited and in the last half of 1976 the 1st deployed four times away from Langley for periods of 30 days each.

Some risks were being taken in trying to meet the situation head on. That first deployment was made only 17 days after the arrival of the 24th aircraft at Langley, but Red Flag exercises at Nellis AFB, NV proved an ideal environment to make up in training realism the shortcomings of sortie generation and capability.

The engines continued to place the largest demand on the maintenance effort, with about 15 MMH/FH or almost half the total maintenance effort. This is actually five times the propulsion maintenance expended in the single engine F-16. Even on a per-engine basis the F100 in the F-16 requires less than half the manhours of the same engine in the F-15, apparently due to the smoother flow experienced in the F-16's underfuselage, fixed geometry inlet. While there were gradual improvements in the MBTF of the propulsion system, fuel pump and fuel control failures, plus stalls and stagnations continued to wreak havoc on the overall system performace. Stalls and stagnation problems proved to be exceptionally stubborn in spite of everything that was done.

The fire control/radar system improved during 1976 with many hardware and software fixes. The system includes a build-in test (BIT) capability that isolates failures in any one of the 99 line replaceable units (LRU) or black boxes installed in the aircraft. The failed unit was to be removed and replaced, or if no spares were available to base supply, removed, repaired and replaced. The problem was that an average of only 48% were actually repaired at base level. The remainder went back to the contractor for repair because the AIS test stations were down for extended periods, averaging less than 50% availability.

This Avionics Intermediate Shop (AIS), composed of six test stations, was available to the maintenance technicians who removed the black box from the aircraft, plugged it into the appropriate test station and then got a printout or other indication telling which unit in the box to replace to get the system back into service. However, the validation of component test requirements didn't prove credible until the configuration of production avionics had become stabilised. This resulted in intermediate level avionics maintenance lagging behind the delivery of the first production aircraft by more than two years. Regardless, the maintenance men were coping and they were doing a fine job as well in keeping the aircraft airborne.

Even after production stabilisation, the AIS test equipment fails to agree with the on-board BIT in over 40% of suspected failures. The AIS problem has become a serious bottleneck in readiness and deployability of the F-15. The high failure rate of F-15 electronics and the high cost per part has made it impractical to operate an F-15 base without an AIS, thus increasing the deployment load and requiring extra specialists to operate and repair the AIS.

Pilot training turned out to be the easiest of the tasks due to the quality of people selected for assignment to the 1st Tac Fighter Wing. As the Wing began to increase in personnel and aircraft in January 1976, the programme was to have an average of eight aircraft per month delivered. As the aircraft arrived fairly rapidly, virtually every pilot and all but 75 of the maintenance personnel would have to be brought from zero F-15 experience to fully qualified status. Pilot selection criteria caused much controversy. Proposals varied from accepting normal pilots to selecting a completely hand-picked bunch that would come from a limited number of candidates with extensive air superiority experience. However, the need for a rapid build up of pilots and the limited training resources forced the Wing to make the conversion course as short as possible.

A selection prerequisite was set of at least 250 hours fighter time. Those organising the training thought that highly experienced F-4 pilots would do a bit better than pilots from other aircraft because of their familiarity with radar air combat tactics and the air-to-air mission in general. As things turned out, experience revealed that a pilot's background in a specific fighter was not as important as his adaptability and learning capability. When all was said and done, selections became very subjective and finding the best men for the job became, as it always is, a matter of personal recommendation and job records.

Even more difficult to select were the senior NCO maintenance specialists in charge of quality control, plans and scheduling, and mobility. There was no way to identify the experience that personnel had in these specific areas. Again it came to selection based on personal contact with former supervisors. Everyone felt that this was a questionable approach at best, but it was the only one they had.

As of 1980, skilled NCO maintenance specialists were still the most critical shortage in operational

Right: As 1976 began, the F-15 was in the process of being tested in the air-to-ground role. The aircraft was cleared for delivery up to 700kts and from 0.5g to 7.33g with seven tons of ordnance. The Eagle's computer proved quite accurate in this role, on par with the best air-to-surface aircraft in the inventory. *MCAIR*

Above right: Bombed up and ready to go as air-to-surface tests gathered momentum in early 1976. Note that no air-to-air ordnance has been removed from the aircraft. *MCAIR*

Below right: A good look at a TF-15 (later redesignated F-15B) hung with air-to-ground ordnance and Sparrow missiles. *MCAIR*

F-15 wings, due primarily to the heavy demands for highly skilled personnel.

By February 1975 the 58th TFTW at Luke was deliberately overmanned by as much as 133% so that personnel could be generated while keeping the first operational wing 100% manned.

The pilots selected for the 1st Wing were sent to an initial 21-sortie programme with the 'Triple Nickel' at Luke. A sortie production rate of 0.9 sorties per aircraft per training day was required to meet the needs of the F-15 conversion check-out programme and the Follow-on Operational Test and Evaluation (FOT&E) programme at Luke. After a few months of operation in 1974, however, it was clear contractor maintenance practices and bookkeeping during development and initial operational testing resulted in an overly optimistic forecast of initial sortie production capability within TAC. There was no way the programme would produce enough pilots in the amount of time allotted.

Things were adjusted a bit so that 0.7 SPR could be flown to train the pilots while the operational test aircraft continued to fly 0.9. This would be a way of life resulting in a continuing sortie until both the spares and reliability situation could be improved.

Throughout 1975 TAC was still trying to achieve pilot production goals. In November 1975, a major decision was made to eliminate testing and training for the Eagle's other role, the air-to-ground mission. Difficulties had developed in the F-15's air-to-ground weapons compatability ('Seek Eagle') as well as shortages in pilot training sorties. Therefore, the air-to-ground attack portions of the syllabus were deleted for Class 76 BCL and subsequent classes. Thus, the F-15 is the first USAF fighter since World War 2 to have no air-to-ground role. Programmed flying training goals were reduced again to a 0.65 SPR, based on the first collected operational data.

In March 1976 several of the classes were slipped and in April the AIMVAL/ACEVAL tests siphoned off six specially configured F-15s and a substantial number of training sorties, 262 to be exact. By early May the overall impact of the programme amounted to the loss of 14 pilots from the 1st Fighter Wing.

Phase two training began at Langley after the pilots had arrived from Luke. Each pilot was scheduled for 25 to 30 sorties over a 75-day period, which included three basic fighter manoeuvre, six air combat manoeuvre, one defensive basic flight manoeuvre, three dissimilar aircraft combat tactics, one night air refuelling and four air defence sorties. There was also a seven-sortie local upgrading instructor pilot programme which gave the Wing enough IPs to support its additional training load. As it was, some of the pilots ended up graduating several sorties short.

The first six upgrade pilot training students started their F-15 check outs on 28 June 1976 and graduated on 23 November after completing 52 effective training sorties (or 10 sorties per month), a 30-sortie increase over the standard conversion check out for previous fighters.

By the end of 1976 the Wing was to have two squadrons of mission-ready pilots and by the end of 1977, a total of six squadrons of mission-ready pilots were to be available. The extra three squadrons would form the 36th Tac Fighter Wing which would deploy to Bitburg, Germany under Operation 'Ready Eagle'.

Looking back on this task it becomes quite an amazing example of just how hard the Wing worked to meet its goals. Every sortie had to be extremely effective in what it taught its pilot. Specific one-versus-two and two-versus-two combat scenarios were formulated to measure pilot proficiency. The first estimate based on the first five pilots to enter phase two training was that 40 sorties – 18 at Luke and 22 at Langley – would bring most pilots to the desired level. It fell to the 27th Tactical Fighter Squadron to develop a detailed pilot training flow plan. Then the 71st and the 94th Squadrons in turn developed their own flow plans as they started flying operations. Due to the need for at least one fully operational F-15 squadron, a decision was made not to disperse 27th Squadron experience, but some cross feeding was available when the 27th operations officer was transferred first to the 71st and then assigned as commander of the 94th upon its activation on 1 August.

Since Langley is on the Atlantic coast the ranges out over the water were used extensively by the Wing. With the initial portion of each range mission being devoted to air defence training, ground control intercept (GCI) was provided on almost all flights. To provide enough targets and training F-4Es and B-52s from Seymour Johnson AFB, North Carolina and EB-57s from Burlington, Vermont, served as dart ships, deception jammers and noise jammers.

Below: After the 1st Wing became fully operational in 1976, it was tasked to get the 36th TFW ready for deployment to Bitburg, Germany. This is a view of Langley in early 1977 before the mass flight of 23 Eagles across the Atlantic. The BT birds can be seen in the background. *MCAIR*

Dissimilar air combat training (DACT) was provided in initial checkouts against the F-5 equipped Aggressor Squadron from Nellis AFB. With these sorties pilots were finally beginning to find out what the F-15 could do against a smaller, very manoeuvrable target similar to the MiG-21. Since every sortie was to be effective there were no cross countries of 'flying around the flagpole' to build flying time. The Eagle drivers found themselves going against Air Force and Navy T-38s, Air Force F-5Es and F-4Es, Navy A-4s, Air Force F-106s and Marine and Navy F-4Js. By the end of January 1977 a total of 528 DACT sorties had been generated by the F-15s.

As pilots became more familiar with the aircraft all the training pivoted around the two air-to-air Designated Operational Capabilities (DOCs) for the Wing . . . air superiority and air defence. Special emphasis was given to the tactical target scenario expected in the European theatre. With this Phase 3 was finally introduced and divided into three categories: (1) Mission Ready – pilot ready for immediate introduction into combat; (2) Mission Capable – pilot capable of performing the mission, but requiring additional training as determined by the unit commander; (3) Basic Proficiency – pilot qulified to fly the F-15.

When the pilots went out to Red Flag at Nellis they found that operational and maintenance readiness accelerated rapidly and everything they were learning came into play as they simulated being in an actual forward combat location.

The first Red Flag deployment took place on 6 July 1976 only 58 days after the receipt of the 24th aircraft at Langley. Red Flag scenarios for the Eagle were structured around the air-to-air DOCs, including a variety of roles – air defense fighters, fighter, CAP/ Escort, airfield/air defence and composite strike.

By 11 September the Wing sent 24 aircraft to Red Flag VIII and for the first time the 1st was able to produce a regular 1.0 SPR. Into the beginning of 1977 the unit found itself undertaking almost every type of mission that the Eagle had been slated for and pilots were becoming happier with what they were able to do. The higher level of sorties generated was laid directly at the feet of maintenance training when the training was often very hard to get. A good example of this was TACs' receipt of its first F-15 with completely unproven engine diagnostic equipment. As training proceeded it became obvious that the task of building from a cadre of 75 F-15 experienced maintenance technicians and managers to over 1,200 qualified people would overwhelm training capability using traditional approaches. As a result, the Wing decided to expand the use of instructional system development techniques and task oriented training was implemented by May 1976. This was another fine example of meeting the situation with what was available regardless of the obstacles.

When the 15th F-15 arrived on 31 March 1976 there were only 27 quality control personnel assigned. Even though they were considered well qualified in their technical field, only three had 'hands-on' experience with the aircraft. Furthermore, only 15 of the 27 had previous quality control experience at all. These dedicated ground-pounders were faced with the challenge of making sure weapon systems maintenance met the need while simultaneously training their own numbers in quality control functions, and on the F-15 weapons systems.

When all the maintenance was looked at everyone became painfully aware that two maintenance activities would be the source of continuing problems: the Avionics Intermediate Shop and F100 engine maintenance. The AIS depends heavily on the computerised test stations which failed so frequently that enough units weren't available. By the end of 1975 the last month before arrival of the first Eagle at Langley, the total AIS operational capability was only 29%.

The F100 engine was the most complex engine ever used in a fighter, and the F-15 engine diagnostic equipment and handling/servicing ground equipment failed to develop along with the engine. There were two major reasons for this: first, a lack of developer, user and supplier agreement on what constituted 'on-condition' maintenance and adequate diagnostic ground equipment; second, the engine contract as interpreted by the Joint Engine Project Office (JEPO) did not require Pratt & Whitney to demonstrate performance reliability and maintainability of the proposed production ground equipment in Contractor Development Test and Evaluation/Air Force Development Test and Evaluation stages. P&WA had been allowed to support the engines for the flight test evaluation programme with their ground equipment meeting their needs, but not necessarily the ground equipment that would be provided for operational use. Impressive engine change times of much less than 30 minutes were demonstrated but people said this was certainly not an example of what would happen when the engine entered operational service.

Another goal was to make the engine operate satisfactorily throughout the useable F-15 flight envelope without stall, afterburner blowout, rumble, in flight starting problems, fluctuating oil pressure, or other problems. The engine still suffers from slow acceleration, unreliable afterburner light, blowouts at slow speed and difficult in-flight restarting. But most serious is the stubborn problem of engine stagnation characterised by loss of thrust, decreasing rpm and rapid increase of turbine inlet temperature. These overtemperatures, in turn, lead to the current short life, excessive inspections and removals, and high rate of replacement of expensive hot section parts such as turbine blades. By October 1976 the overall F100 stall stagnation rate was still 5.5 per 1,000 engine flying hours.

Just getting a wing to operational readiness would have been enough of a challenge but by the end of 1976 the 1st Tac Fighter Wing was not only manned, housed, trained and ready to deploy and fight, but was tasked to assist the first F-15 wing in USAFE, the 36th, to attain operational readiness. The goal was to provide the Bitburg Wing with trained operational and maintenance personnel required to attain readiness status with only a theatre checkout remaining. The end result was to see three USAFE F-15 squadrons for NATO all-weather air superiority and air defense missions by the end of 1977. All the squadrons would be formed at Langley and then deployed by Bitburg when operationally ready. The first 'Ready Eagle' maintenance trainee started hands-on training at Langley in late September 1976 and a monthly flow of maintenance people began subsequently. Incredibly, the desired 522 qualified people were in place at Bitburg by 15 April 1977 ready to receive the first squadron.

The 1st Tac Fighter Wing was to provide flying training with 38 mission-ready, mission-capable supervisors . . . the first 'Ready Eagle' pilot achieved mission-ready status on 14 January 1977. To ensure first squadron readiness at Bitburg, TAC decided that squadron composition would be made up of a mix with half of the experienced F-15 pilots transferring from Langley and Luke and the other half coming from Bitburg. By 25 April 32 pilots, including the Wing Commander and a squadron commander, were fully qualified and ready to deploy.

The 36th Wing Commander, Brig-Gen Fred Kyler, was enjoying the task of getting his aircraft and men ready. It was the capstone to an excellent career. The 94th Squadron served as the parent unit for Ready Eagle and pilots upon graduation from Luke or Nellis came directly into the Squadron while USAFE pilots were given a 20 to 25 sortie phase two upgrade training programme. Included in this were 25 of the USAFE pilots who participated in a full Red Flag training cycle. As with anything this involved, there were a rash of complications including a slow down in

Left: The 1st Wing flight line in May 1977, Langley AFB, Virginia. *MCAIR*

Above: A four-ship flight of F-15As from Langley over Kitty Hawk, North Carolina, November 1977. *USAF*

Centre right: Eagles from Langley pull up to take on fuel from an EC-135, an electronically packed Stratotanker used to direct the deployment of USAF aircraft. *USAF*

Bottom right: Langley before the Eagles of 36th TFW deployed to Bitburg, Germany. *MCAIR*

delivery of aircraft from the depot installing the ECM gear and a rash of catastrophic failures in the latest configuration engine fuel pumps. By the end of March, TAC declared these pumps unsuitable for the seven-hour deployment flight to Bitburg. Because of the complexity of a night launch and rendezvous, the entire operation was practised on the night of 20 April.

At 0353 EST on 27 April the first cell of three Eagles with two air spares began the deployment for Bitburg Air Base. The three remaining cells followed at 30-minute intervals. By 1600 local time in Germany that first cell of Ready Eagles touched down after several aerial refuellings on the way. The 1st Wing had done a remarkable job of getting not only itself but the 36th Wing ready for combat operations.

The Eagle began to stretch its muscles a bit more when in 1976 the aircraft went against two non-manoeuvring Bomarc jet drones, intended to simulate MiG-25 interceptors. The first encounter saw an Eagle launch an AIM-7F Sparrow missile at a Bomarc travelling at Mach 2.7 at 71,000ft. The missile, though armed with a dummy warhead, was judged to have passed within 'lethal distance' of the target. On the second engagement, this time with an Eagle carrying live Sparrow missiles, a Bomarc flying at 68,000ft, again at a speed of Mach 2.7, was destroyed with a launch of one Sparrow. Aircraft and crews taking part in tests came from the AF Test and Evaluation Center at Luke AFB.

More tests have been done at China Lake Naval Weapons Test Center, California, Eglin AFB, Florida and White Sands, New Mexico. The tests have shown that the newest Sparrow, the AIM-7F, has, just like previous Sparrows, severe problems against manoeuvring targets, off-the-beam targets and targets at low altitude or in ground clutter.

McDonnell and the Air Force decided to stretch the Eagle's legs in late 1976 when the red, white and blue Bicentennial Eagle, a TF-15, flew to four different continents, logged over 34,000 miles, spent well over 100 hours in the air, and averaged more than one flight per day while flying every scheduled mission, all during a 2.5-month period. The mission started in early September when an Air Force crew took off from Lambert St Louis International Airport for Europe. Some 3,840 nautical miles and 7.7 hours later the F-15 landed in England where it performed at the Farnborough Air Show and subsequently

Left: A 36th TFW bird over Europe in 1977. *USAF*

Right: Hardened shelters are a way of life in Europe. This F-15A at Bitburg could potentially survive an attack to get airborne, assuming the runway was intact. *USAF*

Below: The Bicentennial Eagle, TF-2, in June 1978. This F-15 made an extensive Pacific tour after visiting Europe. The countries visited are represented by flags on the nose and names on the tail. The globe traces the aircraft's route of flight. Note the cameras mounted on the underside of the wing and tail to record bomb release tests. One can also see the direct copy of the USAF Thunderbirds' paint scheme. *MCAIR*

visited the USAF base at RAF Alconbury, England and Bitburg Air Base in Germany before returning to St Louis. That leg included 41 flights and 47.6 flying hours, logged by Lt-Col John R. Britt, commander of the 94th Tac Fighter Squadron and Capt William L. Hamilton of the 27th TFS, both a part of the 1st Wing at Langley.

One week after arriving back in St Louis the Eagle flew off again, this time for Asia and Australia. The flight log lists 8.3 hours and 3,580 nautical miles to Hawaii and 8.2 hours and 3,361 nautical miles to Yakota Air Base, Japan. Capt Carl Baker of Luke AFB and Lt-Col G. J. Higgs of AFPRO St. Louis were at the controls for the Hickam leg, while Captain Baker flew with Captain Robert Ellis on the leg to Yakota. After flying in the Japan Air Show the Eagle left for Australia. En route the F-15 stopped at Osan and Kunsan AFB in Korea; Kadena Air Base, Okinawa; and Clark Air Base in the Philippines. The stops were made to demonstrate the aircraft to Pacific Air Force commanders.

The circuitous route to Australia involved almost 14 hours in the air and about 5,400 nautical miles. After arrival at the Royal Australian Air Force Base at Williamtown, the Eagle logged 19 flights in six flying days. As many as five flights per day were flown. One mission, covering 1,844 nautical miles from Perth in the west to Williamtown in the east, made the F-15 the first fighter to fly nonstop and unrefuelled across the continent. The Australian visit included nine air shows, four air-to-ground demonstration flights with 17 MK-82 500lb bombs aboard, five air combat manoeuvring flights with Mirage III fighters, and three long range ferry flights. Each scheduled flight was made and no significant maintenance problems arose. During the hectic days in Australia, according to MCAIR sources, technicians were required to change only two black boxes on the airplane. In all, the Asian-Australian leg covered over 26,000 miles including the return flight from Australia to St Louis via Guam, Hawaii, and Luke AFB.

Left: October 1976 – Husband and wife Crew Chiefs, Barry and Sue Lewis, assigned to the 1st Organizational Maintenance Squadron at Langley, went to Red Flag VIII with their Eagles. *USAF*

Below left: Red Flag VIII was a fine example of the 1st TFW's ability to let the Eagle perform after becoming operational the same year. Here maintenance specialists solve a problem at Nellis AFB, Nevada. Note the distinctive 'bare' MCAIR national insignia. *USAF*

Below: S/Sgt Galen Brubaker, a weapons specialist with the 1st Munitions Maintenance Squadron at Langley, prepares an F-15 at Nellis during Red Flag VIII on October 1976. *USAF*

At that time, since its first flight in October 1973, this TF-15 had accumulated 776 flight hours in 626 flights, making it the highest time Eagle with about 50% more flight time than active TAC F-15s.

By January 1977 143 aircraft had been delivered, flying 25,031 flight hours in 19,626 flights. 51 of the aircraft were at Luke in the 58th Tac Fighter Training Wing, 63 at Langley in the 1st Wing, 2 at Nellis in the 57th Fighter Weapons Wing and the factory in St Louis was turning out nine Eagles a month.

The 1st at Langley had been doing a great deal of muscle stretching for the Eagle. Besides being the prime unit in Red Flag VIII from 11 September to 9 October 1976, the unit took part in two large scale air combat training exercises with the E-3A. The first test took place from 6 to 12 November 1976 at Luke AFB with 28 F-15s and 30 pilots deployed. The second exercise was conducted at McChord AFB, when eight aircraft and pilots were deployed from 6 to 9 December.

The exercise out of Luke was, at the time, the most massive and complex tactical air operation ever launched in peacetime by TAC with almost 450 aircraft in the air to help test and evaluate the E-3A, the Air Force's new Airborne Warning and Control System (AWACS). The F-15s were among the defending forces assigned to the AWACS along with more than 40 fighter aircraft assigned to the 58th Wing. The exercise was held over the Edwards AFB and Nellis AFB training areas, as Col John F. O'Donnell, Vice Commander of the 58th, acted as commander of the friendly Blue Forces.

'The scenario we developed,' the Colonel said, 'closely approximated the type of air battle we could expect in a future conflict where we would be faced with a very large number of adversary aircraft.' For the test Col O'Donnell was allotted one AWACS to control the air battle and approximately 120 fighters as well as electronic and aerial tanker support. To form this force the 28 Eagles from the 1st Wing deployed nonstop to Luke where they joined four F-15s and 38 F-4s as part of the Blue Forces. Additional forces flew directly into the test air space from their home bases in Californa, Arizona, Nebraska and Washington. Friendly combat air patrol (CAP) flights were organised into four aircraft each, two F-15s and two F-4s. 'This enabled us to take advantage of the F-15's superior radar and weapons as well as the very effective air-to-air weapons carried by the F-4,' Col O'Donnell explained.

When the 'enemy' attack came it was massive and strong. The Red Forces hit in three waves of approximately 100 aircraft each with the waves separated by 15 minutes. As soon as AWACS detected the attack, the 17-man crew aboard began controlling friendly fighters along with detecting and tracking enemy fighters. Some 50 minutes after the first attack, the test was over.

Naturally the exercise was labelled a success but there were many problems encountered, one being the AWACS requirement of transponder operation in the friendly aircraft. If transponder or IFF (Identification Friend or Foe) was inoperative, then the friendly aircraft became just another blip, making it very difficult to separate friendly from enemy traffic. Even with IFF, control of multiple aircraft dogfights proved difficult. Regardless, pilots and crew were delighted to receive realistic training in the many-on-many environment.

In spite of some accidents and engine problems that continued to plague the F-15, the aircraft was racking up a significant safety record as 1977 wore on. One of the F-15's safety factors was centred on the twin engine aircraft being, supposedly, historically safer than single engine aircraft according to US Air Force and Navy Statistics.*

*It should be noted that another set of statistics can be gathered to prove the opposite. One study found the F-4s in South-east Asia weren't significantly safer than F-105s where mission risk was roughly equal, and that USAF data is often slanted towards comparing multi-engine bombers with single-engine fighters. Good handling and slow landing speeds are much more important than single vs twin engines as well. Thus, a good single is significantly safer than a poor-handling twin with unreliable engines.

Left: An Eagle takes a bath at Red Flag VIII late 1976. Note that the arrestor hook is down. *USAF*

Right: En route to Holloman. The 58th TTW was responsible for supporting the effort as seen by the 461st TFTS F-15B in the foreground. *USAF*

Below: 49th Wing F-15s touch down at Holloman AFB, New Mexico, 20 December 1977. *USAF*

American fighter and attack aircraft non-combat losses from 1956 to 1973 show an average 17.1 losses per 100,000 flight hours for a single engine aircraft. The twin engine aircraft loss rate was 10.5 per 100,000 hours. A Navy peacetime attrition survey showed that a significantly greater percentage of single engine aircraft were destroyed due to engine mishaps than were twin engine aircraft. Records demonstrate that many aircraft were saved by a second engine. A save is counted when a comparable failure in a single engine aircraft would have proven catastrophic. The highest on the catastrophic mishaps list were the F-100 Super Sabre and the F-104 Starfighter.

Regardless of the controversy over safety statistics, many of the fighter pilots who were involved with the F-15 look historically at those fighters that were twin engined and find that they were never significant air superiority aircraft because of their large size. This debate continues to rage within the Pentagon and within fighter development circles because the F-15 is a large airplane and it can be seen from a greater distance than the smaller F-5, F-104 or F-16.

As of 30 September 1977 245 F-15s had been delivered, flying 58,800 flight hours on 43,900 flights. The 58th Wing at Luke had 50 aircraft; Langley had 76 in the 1st Wing; the 57th Wing had 14 at Nellis; while Bitburg was fully up to steam with 73 aircraft in the 36th Wing. The production rate was still at nine aircraft per month.

By the end of 1977 the 49th Tactical Fighter Wing at Holloman AFB, New Mexico was receiving its new F-15s with the 33rd Wing at Eglin AFB, Florida scheduled to be the next operational Eagle unit. The 555th and 461st Tactical Fighter Training Squadrons were certainly in high gear now, providing men to fly the Eagles in the new wings.

Meanwhile the 57th, under the TAC Fighter Weapons Center at Nellis, had the 422nd Fighter Weapons Squadron engaged in Follow-on Operation Test and Evaluation work, formerly known as Category III, to maintain on-going test work, and the 433rd Fighter Weapons Squadron of instructors who produce men trained in the F-15's capabilities, the F-15 tactics experts. One graduate from the 433rd was to be placed in each squadron of F-15s as it was activated. The 433rd's first class began in January of 1978. Even though the classes were small with only four to six students per class and three classes a year, these men were to transfer their knowledge back to line units.

In January 1977 the F-15 became involved in a Department of Defense test programme called AIMVAL/ACEVAL. Both the Navy and the Air Force were after tests that would evaluate current and future missiles, analysed on the Air Combat Manoeuvring Instrumentation range at Nellis. The AIMVAL portion stood for Air Intercept Missile while the ACEVAL portion was to test combinations of aircraft and explore the impact of numbers on visual air-to-air combat under various GCI conditions. F-14s were also thrown into the picture and computers were linked up to track the potential capabilities even though nothing was fired. The F-14s and F-15s in the Blue Force went against the Red Force F-5Es from the aggressor squadrons out of Nellis.

Many improvements were made as a result to help the pilot keep his head out of the cockpit with such things as a visual identification target acquisition system (VITAS), in essence a helmet-mounted eye piece, that activated the weapon system when placed on target, and lights on the canopy rail, one to tell the pilot that the radar is locked on the other to indicate that he is in the envelope for both the AIM-7F and the AIM-9L missiles.

The tests, which lasted for about 10 months, were not only fascinating in that they placed air combat back where it was supposed to be, pilot versus pilot, but they also tested weapons capabilities at the hands of pilots who were placed at first in one-versus-one, and then one-versus-many and many-versus-many scenarios. (See Chapter 7 for a more detailed appraisal of AIMVAL/ACEVAL.)

Throughout 1977 the 36th Wing at Bitburg was gaining strength but it was clear that NATO and USAF in Europe (USAFE) planners wanted more Eagles to overcome the numerical superiority of the Warsaw Pact air forces. On 13 September 1978 the 1st Tac Fighter Wing culminated another mission in support of getting combat ready F-15s into NATO. After months of planning on both sides of the Atlantic, the 'Coronet Sandpiper' deployment resulted in 16 F-15s of the 1st Wing's 71st Squadron, accompanied by the first two Eagles to be assigned to the 32nd Tac Fighter Squadron, entering the landing pattern at Camp New Amsterdam (Soesterberg) Royal Netherlands Air Base. This new USAFE F-15 squadron would now operate from a Dutch base under NATO control.

For three months the 1st Wing's pilots assisted the 32nd, led by 71st commander Lt-Col Jon I. Lucas, who also served as deployment commander. Operational transfer of the F-15s from the Tactical Air Command to the US Air Forces in Europe took

Above right and below right: Bodo AS, Norway during 'Arctic Express' 17 February-12 March 1978. The 36th deployed to the north during a multi-national combat readiness exercise under arctic conditions. *USAF*

Left: 49th Wing F-15s.

Below: Two F-15As taxi out for a sortie at Bitburg, Germany. *USAF*

place when Col Neill Eddins, 1st Wing Commander, and Col Albert L. Pruden Jr, 32nd Commander, taxied their F-15s into the ceremonial area at Soesterberg and turned their aircraft over to Lt-Gen Benjamin N. Bellis, USAFE Vice Commander. Just over a month later on 15 December the 33rd Tac Fighter Wing received its first Eagles at Eglin AFB.

Eagle deployments were becoming a way of life, particularly for the 1st Wing. On 20 January 1979 a dozen F-15s of the 94th Tac Fighter Squadron deployed to Saudi Arabia. Unofficially, this was a political show of support for the Saudis. Officially, the Air Force had been invited by the Saudis to demonstrate the performance characteristics and capabilities of the F-15 since they had ordered 60 Eagles for delivery in the early 1980s. This deployment was made, incidentally, just after the 94th had returned from its 54-day deployment to Soesterberg. 'We were home about long enough to wash our socks and balance the checkbook,' said Lt-Col John L. Borling, Squadron Commander. But with less than 72 hours' notice the famous 'Hat-in-the-Ring Squadron' was on its way again across the Atlantic on 13 January, although quite a number of F-15s were needed to get six deployed.

About 200 other specialists from the 1st Wing accompanied the deployment aboard C-141s and C-5s as the six F-15s arrived at Khmis Mishayt Royal Saudi Air Force Base near the north Yemen border. The Eagles, after a nine-hour flight from Lajes Field, Azores, arrived in the capital city of Riyadh to be greeted by Saudi Arabia's Deputy Prime Minister, Crown Prince Fahd Bin Abdul Aziz, US Ambassador John C. West and a number of other Saudi officials.

On 17 January the six Eagles at Riyadh flew to Khmis Mishayt closing ranks with the rest of the deployed aircraft. From that base the detachment flew several orientation flights, hosted static displays and made 'out-and-back' visits to Taif and Jedda near Mecca.

A number of training sorties were generated between F-15s and the RSAF F-5s. Saudi pilots who had an opportunity to fly in the F-15 were naturally quite pleased with the possibility of flying the aircraft. It was a unique deployment. All involved, both on the ground and in the air, were treated royally while thoroughly enjoying the hospitality and the opportunity to perform their mission in a new environment.

The five women of the 1st Wing who made the deployment became the first women of any nationality to dine at the Officer's Club of the Saudi Arabian Air Force at Khmis Mishayt. To say the least, it was a precedent-breaker among the Saudis who have very strict customs concerning their women.

The redeployment phase began on 22 January as the Langley detachment split into three groups to stage through Sudan, Morocco and Spain. The detachment re-joined on 25 and 26 January at Montijo Air Base near Lisbon, Portugal. At 9am on 27 January the 12 Eagles thundered down a rain-soaked runway and were airborne, landing 8½ hours later at Langley after refuelling from KC-135s. Master Sergeant Aubrey W. Cason, a maintenance NCO, commented after returning. 'This is the best TDY in my 18 year career.'

On the 23rd and 24th the first known bladder refuelling of F-15s took place at Khartoum. Four of the Eagles had stopped there on the return trip, but the international airport had no stock of the normal JP-4 fuel that the F-15 burns. Jet A gas used by commercial airliners was available and can be burned by the thirsty Eagles in an emergency, but an F-15's

Left: Two Eagles of the 36th on a sortie over Eiffel Province, West Germany, August 1977. *USAF*

Below: Engine test run at Bitburg. *USAF*

Right: In ferry configuration with three auxiliary fuel tanks, F-15As of the 18th Wing fly to Kadena to replace F-4Es. *MCAIR*

F100 engines must be retrimmed for Jet A since energy output is different than JP-4. Two C-141s each carried three 3,000gal bladders of JP-4 to Khartoum from Jedda. Normally that fuel would have been pumped from the bladders into storage tanks or trucks, but since neither was available at Khartoum the F-15s had to be refuelled directly from the bladders. According to one F-15 crew chief, Staff Sergeant Eugene B. Jena, the bladder pumps of this Air Bulk Delivery System have no pressure regulators or filter separators, unlike the equipment on refuelling trucks. 'We had to estimate the amount of fuel in each airplane and go from there,' Sergeant Jena said. Two men from the 86th Supply Squadron at Ramstein Air Base, Germany, conducted the operation.

Tech Sergeant John Deininger said the dicey part of direct refuelling is maintaining enough pressure to open and close the valves in the F-15s tanks without letting the pressure get so high that it blows seals. 'We avoid trouble by opening some of the valves that allow the JP-4 to circulate freely between the ABDS and the F-15.'

The only problem encountered was an inability to top off the tanks completely due to low pressure and lack of familiarity with the equipment. The importance of all this revolved around the F-15's capability to operate from a bare base with C-141 support.

In late 1979 it became the 33rd Wing's turn to get another F-15 unit ready. Under 'Ready Eagle III' pilots from the 18th Tac Fighter Wing's 67th Fighter Squadron at Kadena, Okinawa were trained to fly the F-15 using Eglin's maintenance facilities and people. Since 12 July pilots had been trained to mission ready status and two to mission support status, while another 57 pilots were trained thereafter. On 29

Above and above right: Fully armed F-15s of the 32nd Tactical Fighter Squadron on patrol during August 1979 out of Camp New Amsterdam, Soesterburg AB, Netherlands. *MCAIR*

September the Pacific Air Force (PACAF) received their first F-15 squadron with the arrival of 16 Eagles from Eglin. Three F-15s were already on location. Beginning the previous May, 100 maintenance people had been trained and another 200 scheduled as training for pilots and maintenance people was completed by March 1980.

Delivery of Kadena's entire Okinawa complement of 72 F-15s to replace their F-4s was completed by the end of 1980.

As 1979 drew to a close many problems began to surface that became more and more disturbing as the F-15 attempted to attain operational maturity. Engine fires, high angles of attack, afterburner use and engine stagnation were factors in five of the nine crashes since the aircraft's first flight as of April 1979. Thus, the proportion of engine-related accidents was twice as high as was customary on twin engine aircraft. The Air Force and industry teams jumped into the problem to modify the aircraft's jet fuel starter system to facilitate inflight engine restarts, restricting afterburner use on the F100 engines and reviewing F-15 maintenance procedures. The five aircraft that crashed all belonged to the 36th Wing at Bitburg, the only unit that was to have a maintenance review which ended up with only minor easily correctable discrepancies.

The first European F-15 crash had occured on 17 April 1978 involving an aircraft practising air combat tactics. The pilot reported that he was low on fuel and the report continued 'two minutes later number three said he had a problem and indicated that he had 4,000lb of total fuel but no fuel in the feed tanks. The right engine flamed out followed in two minutes by a left engine flameout. The pilot ejected at about 14,000ft in anticipation of complete loss of flight control.'

Another incident that did not involve a crash took place on 7 June 1978 while the F-15 was performing a NATO cross servicing mission to Hopsten Air Base, Germany. The report said, 'Upon selection of augmentors (afterburners) for a vertical maneuver, the left engine bay fire light illuminated on the instrument panel. After going through the required procedures the aircraft returned to Bitburg and it was found the the left engine and left engine bay had fire damage.'

On 15 June 1978 a pilot ejected after reporting one engine stagnated and the other refusing to start. On 6 July 1978 an aircraft crashed north of Bitburg on an instrument departure, killing the pilot. On 19 December 1978 an F-15 burst into flames during air combat training and the pilot ejected after a wingman reported fire coming from the nozzle area, probably from the right engine.

In trying to find common denominators to many of these incidents, afterburner hard starts were blamed for more than three-quarters of all F100 stagnation stalls.

By late 1979 only 35% of the 1st Tac Fighter Wing's F-15s were listed as fully capable of flying combat missions on any given day, as compared to 50% for the entire complement of 450 F-15's in Tactical Air Command. Although this information was given through the *New York Times* news service, within Pentagon circles many spokesmen have said that the actual readiness rate is lower, primarily due to the cannibalisation of parts to keep other aircraft flying.

Along with the F-111D and F-111A, the overall readiness rate for all US tactical aircraft has come down to 50%.

In 1978 there were 15,474 cannibalisations of parts on the F-15 which consumed 47,898 maintenance manhours. In a Congressional hearing Brig-Gen Richard W. Phillips, Air Force Deputy Director for General Purpose Forces, said, 'While in excess of 47 manhours were expended on cannibalisation actions for the F-15, this effort represents only 2.6% of 1.8million maintenance manhours expended against the F-15 aircraft in 1978.' Both ground crew and pilots at Langley were in a bitter-sweet mood when talking about this. All of them praised the aircraft's performance, but they were clearly unhappy with its maintenance problems. 'Am I nervous flying this plane?' asked one pilot. 'Let's put it this way, I'm very glad it has two engines.'

Air Force spokesmen have been saying that they hope by 1983 or 1984 the situation will be stabilised.

In spite of the problems, the F-15's loss rate as of the end of 1979 had been half that of any previous US fighter at the same point operationally. 1978 was the first year that the F-15 had a chance to be deployed globally. Eagles based at 10 locations in four countries, deployed to 12 other countries including Greece, the UK, Spain, Denmark, Pakistan, Norway, Belgium, Italy, Korea, Japan, the Philippines and Canada.

Deployments aided aircrew training and reinforced the US commitment to its allies in NATO, CENTO and the Pacific. Two bases received F-15s in 1978, the 33rd Tac Fighter Wing at Eglin and the 32nd Fighter Squadron at Camp New Amsterdam, Soesterberg, in the Netherlands. By the end of 1978 F-15s had accumulated 135,000 flight hours.

In testing the F-15's supportability and readiness during 1978, the 36th Wing generated 322 sorties in less than 24 hours with 71 aircraft. In another exercise the 1st Wing flew 636 sorties with 35 F-15s in six days. The year was completed with the lowest loss rate, 7.4 losses per 100,000 flight hours, of any tactical fighter aircraft in recent history.

The Eagle was also tested in airfield defence involving a deployment of a detachment of F-15s to Michael Army Field in Utah to protect that base and Wildcat Air Field, a mock air field with target arrays, from air attack. Minimum intelligence, only the approximate time of attack, was given the F-15 detachments. The aircraft's pilots were able to use its radar and battle management capability as a mini-airborne warning and control system to detect incoming strike aircraft so that other F-15s on ground alert or assigned combat air patrol positions were alerted to intercept the incoming raid.

Today the USSR/Warsaw Pact forces threatening the West appear to outnumber the NATO air forces. New WP aircraft since 1970 are becoming larger and more multi-mission orientated. This has been the primary motivation for stationing much of the F-15 force in Europe. Air Force thinking at present considers the F-15s based in the continental United States as backup aircraft to those stationed in Europe and the Pacific. The USAF would like to buy additional F-15s for strategic air defence of the continental US, but only if the DoD increased the total USAF budget accordingly. This DoD has refused to do, primarily because of the minimal size of the Soviet intercontinental bomber force. In the interim, the USAF has assigned add-on continental air defence duties to the available F-15s in Tactical Air Command.

Eagle Production

Above: Eagle production line in St Louis, October 1974. *MCAIR*

Left: August 1975 – Eagles on the left, Phantoms on the right. As the F-4 reaches toward number 5,000, Eagle F-49 stands in the foreground minus the forward fuselage. *MCAIR*

Above: The St Louis production line in April 1977. TF-32 is in the foreground, and Phantoms in the front row. *MCAIR*

Left: Eagle line as of February 1978. Note three Phantoms up front. *MCAIR*

Below left: McDonnell's flight test hangars, September 1978. From front to rear are the AV-8B test airframe, the first F-18 Hornet, the fourth F-15 and an F-4C Phantom II. *MCAIR*

4. Inside the Eagle

The F-15's fuselage is built in three sections for the convenience of manufacturing and repair, major systems being isolated to each of these three sections. The forward fuselage is built to enhance accessibility to the many black boxes inside. It contains 90% of the avionics equipment and over 85% of the wiring. Six non-structural doors with quick release latches provide access to the avionics.

The centre fuselage contains the mechanical parts of the gun, ammunition drum, Sparrow systems and fuel cells. A truss structure allows the wingloads to be carried around the ducts permitting a lower weight, smaller cross section configuration. The wing torque box is a multicell three-spar structure utlising multi-stiffened skins to carry the bending loads into the fuselage through three pairs of pinned lugs. The twin tail arrangement permits the tail booms to be used for structural support of both vertical fins and horizontal stabilators. The horizontal stabilators are interchangeable as are the rudders. The skins of both the fin and the stabilator are made from boron/epoxy composite for maximum stiffness and minimum weight.

To increase aft fuselage structural efficiency, engine removal/installation is made from the rear of the aircraft. This design feature allows for a continuous titanium structure around both engines at some cost in engine accessibility. The engines are separated by a keeled titanium web which supports the arresting gear.

The fixed geometry wing, employing a conventional airfoil and relatively heavy conical camber is of course considerably simpler than a variable sweep wing. When the F-15 was initially going through its USAF concept formulation phase in the late 1960s, the push among technologists and R&D officials was strong for a variable geometry wing much like that on the F-111 or F-14. At this point, with some hindsight, everyone is quite thankful that Col John Boyd persisted in eliminating the complexity and weight of variable sweep from the F-15 design.

The wing is optimised for Mach 0.9 flight. McDonnell decided to eliminate leading edge devices for enhanced manoeuvring lift, electing to replace them with a strongly cambered larger wing. This trade-off worked out well at Mach 0.9 but added considerable drag in the transonic region. 608sq ft of working wing provided a combat wing loading of 60lb/sq ft, essential for a manoeuvrable fighter; as a side benefit it permits landing speeds of 120kts.

The USAF requirement for high dash speed – Mach 2.5 – dictated a variable geometry inlet to achieve adequately close matching of inlet and engine. The inlet rotates about a pivot point near the lower cowl lip. Capture area and ramp position are varied as a function of Mach number, angle of attack and temperature, providing proper inlet/engine matching, reducing spillage drag through the flight envelope. The variable geometry inlet also reduced performance at subsonic and transonic speeds. There are those who believe this feature was unnecessary considering fuel limits and acceleration time dictate that the aircraft will seldom reach speeds over Mach 1.3 – 1.6 in combat. In fact, there are some who believe the variable geometry inlet of the F-15 makes the stall/stagnation/durability problem much more serious on the F-15 than on the fixed geometry F-16. It is interesting to note that the F-14 has had its variable geometry inlets fixed in one position to alleviate engine problems.

The structural design of the Eagle is based on a fatigue life requirement four times higher than the F-4. Moderate 'g' loads can be pulled with any of the three spars in each wing completely severed.

The hydraulic flight control system actually combines two different linkages, one mechanical, the other electrical. The primary system uses the electrical linkage since it allows increased use of artificial stability. The system can sustain battle damage to the mechanical linkage yet remain totally controllable. The control surfaces themselves consist of the outboard ailerons which have a 20° movement up or down, the horizontal stabilators which move symmetrically for pitch and differentially for additional roll control, and twin rudders on the vertical stabilators.

Right: General arrangement drawing of the F-15 showing lack of snags on the stabilators, unraked wing tips and smaller speed brake. *MCAIR*

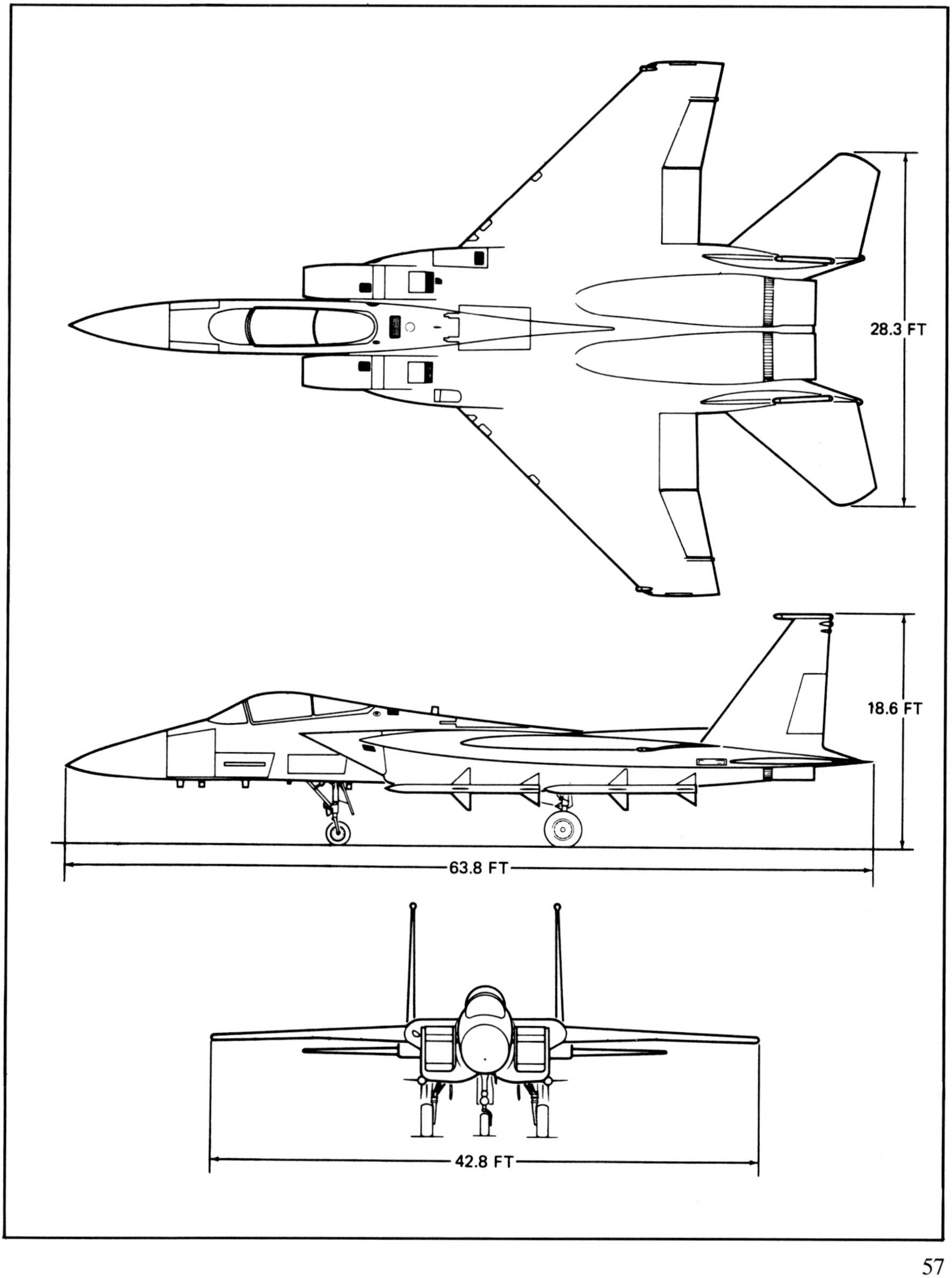
28.3 FT
18.6 FT
63.8 FT
42.8 FT

The heart of all this is the Automatic Flight Control System (AFCS) which provides the Control Augmentation System (CAS) and the autopilot. The CAS receives the pilot's control inputs and converts these to the elctrical inputs to the control surfaces. It senses pitch, roll and yaw rates, vertical and lateral acceleration and angle of attack, and uses these to compute 'correction' to the pilot's input. This reduces the need of compensation increases and decreases in control surface pressure on the pilot's part. The result from the pilot's point of view is an aircraft that does not require a great deal of pushing and shoving at high speed or high 'g'.

The cockpit itself is a welcome reversion to the days of the bubble canopy as mounted on the P-51 and the F-86. It is roomy and obviously designed with good visibility in mind. One sits almost waist high within the canopy giving an excellent forward and rearward field of view; over-the-side visibility would have been better if the cockpit and fuselage were narrower. Cockpit layout has been given some thought. The switches and controls which the pilot frequently uses are situated where he can get at them without having to change hands on the control stick. For example, the Heads-Up Display (HUD), the radio and the transponder controls are directly in front of the pilot on top of the centre instrument panel. Changing frequencies does not force the pilot to look down into the cockpit. On the left console, the pilot takes his hands off the throttles to operate the radar control box, the fuel dump switch, the ILS and TACAN controls, the landing light switch, the subsystem BIT control panel, the auxiliary radio, and the transponder master controls. Significantly the formation and position lights are placed directly behind the throttle quadrant where they can easily be reached.

The front instrument panel features an armament control panel including a gun rate control and a rounds counter, a missile status panel, master arm switch and air-to-ground programming control. The radar scope is situated in the upper left hand corner of the front instrument panel, making an unavoidable drawback since the pilot does have to look back down into the cockpit to see it. Therefore it remains primarily a BVR (beyond visual range) system.

The standard flight director group plus standby altitude, altimeter and airspeed indicators are situated normally in the middle. The engine instruments are to the right, having a digital readout along with the traditional pointer for RPM, EGT and fuel flow. The fuel quantity gauge measures all aircraft fuel, both internal and external and it tells the pilot just exactly how much fuel is left and where it is located within each tank group. Also included is an adjustable bingo pointer, that is, minimum fuel for return to base, which flashes a bingo warning light when this level is reached.

The right console features the engine control switches: the engine master switches, starter switch and generator switches. And the aircraft can be started without external power, if necessary. All the pilot would have to do is pull his own chocks.

The inertial navigation system (INS) control panel is positioned on the right console as well; it permits the pilot to programme up to 12 destinations. The cabin temperature and lighting controls are located in this area. Temperature control in the aircraft has been particularly easy since the system is effective. Once the canopy comes down, the air conditioning

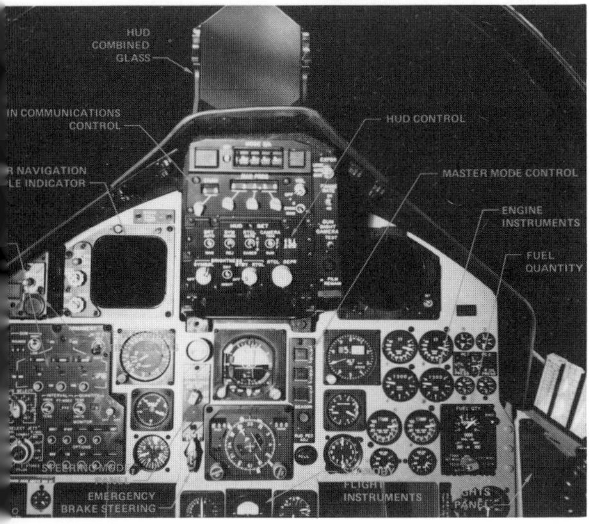

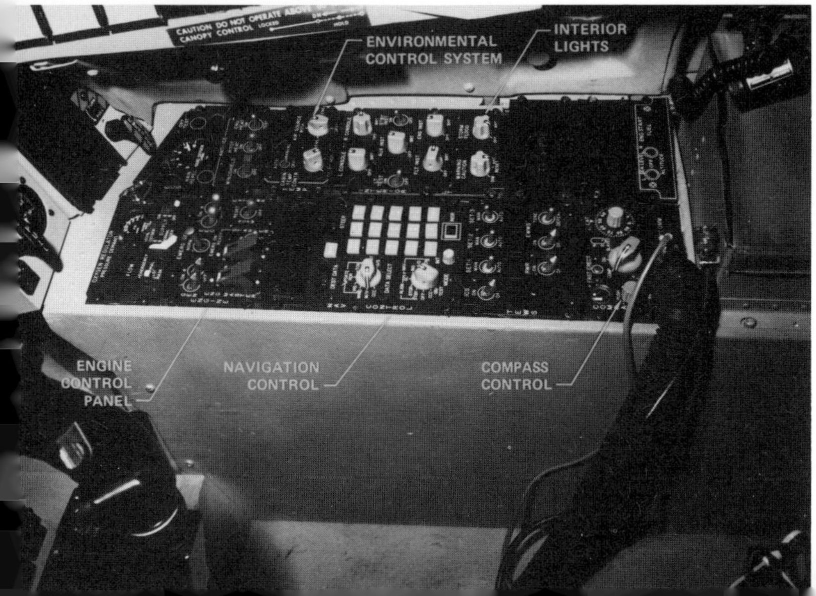

Top far left: Superior cockpit visibility is one of the hallmarks of the Eagle – the sensation is one of sitting out of the aircraft almost waist high. *MCAIR*

Above left and left: Cockpit of the F-15A. *MCAIR*

Above right: McDonnell is continually developing advanced displays for its fighters. This F-15 cockpit has been configured for a newer system of visual ques for the pilot, replacing much of the standard instrumentation. *MCAIR*

system comes on and cabin pressurisation calls for a constant cabin altitude of 8,000ft up to 23,100ft. Above this altitude the regulator maintains a 5lb/sq in differential between cabin and outside pressure. The ACES II ejection seat is operable from zero to 600kts at ground level. To give one an idea of just how fast the pilot can get out in an emergency, from initiation of ejection the rocket on the bottom of the seat ignites 0.3sec later; sustained to 0.45sec, the seat separates at 1.3sec; the parachute pack opens at 2.3sec; and the chute is fully inflated at 4.8 – 6.8sec.

The F-15's throttles and stick are where all the action takes place as far as controlling the aircraft's weapons systems. The right throttle contains the weapon mode selection switch, the speed brake switch, the UHF radio switch and the IFF (transponder) interrogation switch, and the radar target designator control. The latter is what slaves the acquisition gates around on the radar scope and, when the target is bracketed, initiates lock-on when the isometric switch is depressed and released.

The left throttle contains the antenna elevation control and the gun and missile reject switch. Both throttles include fingerlift engine cut-off levers which also initiate engine motoring for engine start when the throttles are in the off position.

One delight from the pilot's point of view is the length of the control stick. Pilots have said that finally somebody's made one long enough so the pilot can play with it a little bit. The buttons on the stick include the AIM-9/nose steering button, the radar mode/refuel button, the trim button, the gun trigger and the weapon release or pickle button, which fires or releases all ordnance except the 20mm cannon. The trigger has a double detent with the first activating the HUD camera (later replaced by a video tape recorder), the second firing the gun.

Although the F-15 has continuous nose wheel steering up to 15° either side, the nose gear steering button gives the pilot a manoeuvre mode of 45° of nose wheel deflection for taxying in tight areas. In flight the nose wheel steering button also uncages and slaves the AIM-9 seeker head.

The air refuelling disconnect button is still on the stick, working when the radar is in 'off' or 'standby'. It is a four-position switch which is spring loaded to a neutral position. Pushing it forward commands the radar into a bore sight mode in which the radar will lock on to the first detected target within 10 miles range. Pulling the button aft commands the radar into super search mode in which the radar rapidly scans the 20° HUD field of view. In super search the radar also automatically locks on to the first detected target, the pilot steering the Eagle to put the HUD on the target. Compressing the switch with the radar in

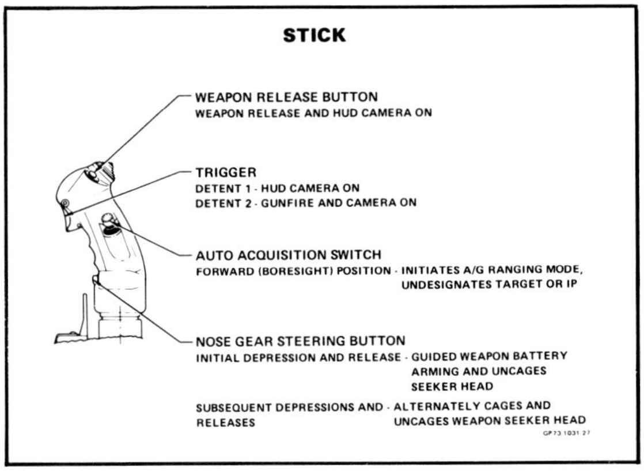

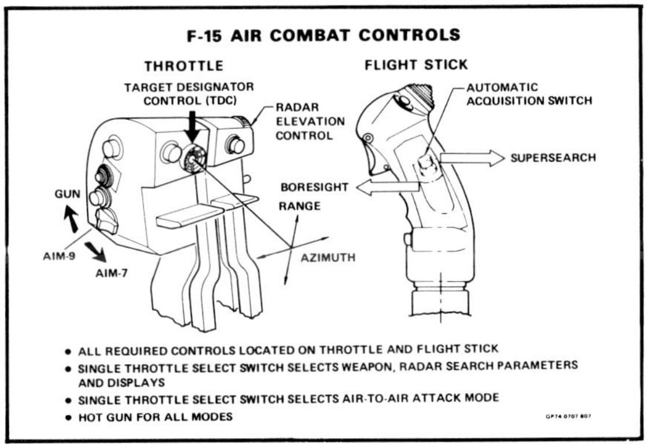

operate breaks any radar lock and returns it to the selected search mode (there are also long range search and tactical search medium PRF modes). Certainly this is complex. However, offsetting the throttle/stick complexity is the fact that there are 30% fewer gauges than in the F-4 and nothing that is needed in flight is behind the pilot's elbows.

The Eagle normally carries 11,635lb of fuel internally (for a 27% fuel fraction). Three external 600gal tanks plus the Fuel and Sensor Tactical packs can up the fuel to a 2,650-nautical mile range for ferry flights. Even though the F-15 is a large airplane by any standards the FAST packs make room for more avionics in addition to fuel. The FAST pack fuel can be reduced to provide space for interceptor systems with data link, infra-red search and track, TISEO (target identification system electro optical) gear, or it can be modified for reconnaissance with cameras, data link, JTIDS (Joint Tactical Information Data System) and photo flash. Or strike assist with a laser designator, low light level TV, forward looking infra-red radar and Loran. SAM suppression is also in the picture with additional electronic support measures, tactical jamming equipment and chaff.

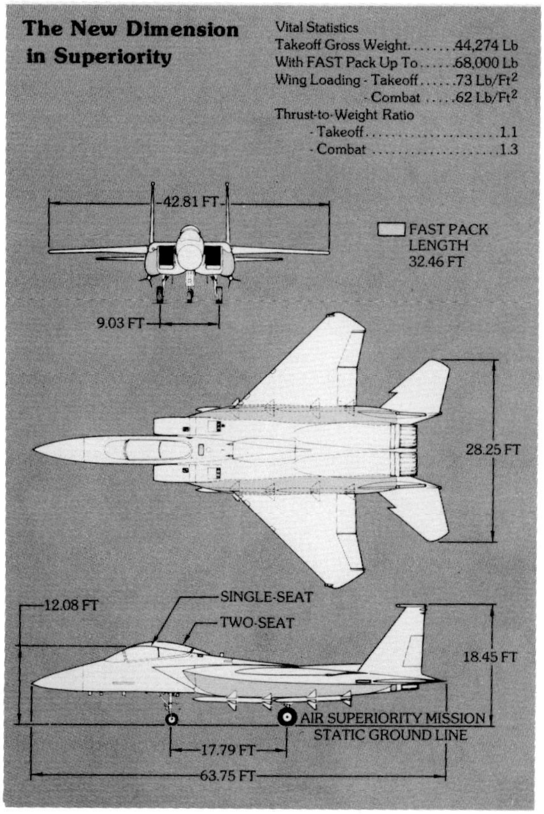

The FAST packs are said by MCAIR actually to improve the aerodynamics of the aircraft subsonically although this has been questioned by others.

The avionics and weapon systems in the Eagle must be considered as an integrated unit since each was designed for the other as a package for the aircraft. The heart of this system is the central computer which is capable of performing 340,000 instructions per second, weighing only 48.5lb. This computer was intended to automate many radar and fire control functions to avoid adding a second seat and weapons operator. In simplified form, the system assists three functions: look – select – fire.

Look: The Vertical Situation Display (VSD) gives radar range and azimuth and presents targets artificially with a dot on a 'clean' scope without the clutter of a normal radar scope. The result is easy to

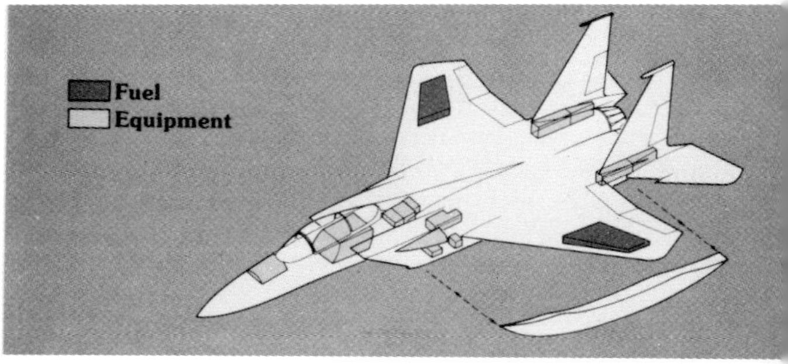

Above left: Why an Eagle pilot must educate his hands to fly the aircraft. *MCAIR*

Above and above right: The FAST pack. *MCAIR*

Right: F-15A external stores leading.

F-15A EXTERNAL STORES LOADING

STORES	WEIGHT (LB)	9	8	7	6	5	4	3	2	1	TOTAL
AIR-TO-AIR MISSILES											
• AIM-7F	510			1	1		1	1			4
• AIM-9E/L	168/195		2						2		4/4
GENERAL PURPOSE/DEMOLITION BOMBS											
• MK-82 SLICK	527		6			6			6		18
• MK-82 SNAKEYE	560		6			6			6		18
• MK-84 SLICK	1970		1			1			1		3
FIRE BOMBS											
• BLU-27B/B (FINNED AND UNFINNED)	814/799		3			3			3		9/9
GUIDED BOMBS											
• MK-84 LASER	2052		1			1			1		3
• MK-84 EO	2276		1			1			1		3
• MK-84 IR	2123		1			1			1		3
DISPENSERS											
• CBU-52B/B	785		4			4			4		12
• CBU-58/B	820		4			4			4		12
• CBU-71/B	820		4			4			4		12
• MK-20 ROCKEYE	490		6			6			6		18
TRAINING											
• SUU-20B/A	455		1			1			1		3
FUEL TANK											
• 600 GALLON	4285		1			1			1		3
TEWS PODS	440	1								1	2

GP74-4541-55

Above: An AIM-7 has just been launched. Through the HUD the pilot has the missile (and possibly the target) in sight through the target acquisition box. From the top, clockwise, the pilot can read the following: magnetic heading of 098°, pressure altitude (not visible here), relative speed of target 55kts, pitch reference line 5° below horizon, speed of F-15 is Mach 0.976 and pulling 1.0g, calibrated airspeed is 342kts. The steering circle in the centre shows, from the top, a gun cross, a reticle with a steering dot and aircraft fore and aft axis. The flight path or velocity vector of the F-15 is shown by the circle with fin and wings just outside the steering circle on the lower right. *MCAIR*

read, but at times difficult to interpret in the presence of jamming or moving ground targets. In the search mode the radar will lock on to targets, automatically or manually, in the forward quadrant above or below the Eagle. Target range, speed, g being pulled and aspect (such as 170 degrees left) also reads out digitally on the scope. Once the pilot has interpreted the radar display and locked on, the HUD allows the pilot to look outside while giving speed, bearing, altitude, g, Mach number, course and altitude of his own aircraft. A steering dot on the HUD tells the pilot where to point the aircraft toward the target and a target designator box surrounds the target position on the glass so one's eyes are directed right at the spot in the sky where the target is flying. Then it tells when the selected weapons, if fired, will kill the target.

Select: Radar mode control and weapons select are on the throttle, the pilot possibly having to change between various radar modes to resolve ambiguities or false targets on the scope.

Fire: The trigger and weapon release button on the stick complete the sequence.

Since the F-15 is an air superiority fighter all subsystems are automatically set in the air-to-air mode unless some other mode is manually selected. In this case air-to-air is reselected in one step by placing the weapons select switch on the throttle to the guns position. The pilot, however, is in no way limited to the guns in his weapons selection. Once the weapon select switch has been positioned to guns, all previous manual selections are overridden. The pilot is then free to select either AIM-7s, AIM-9s, or he can, of course, leave the weapon switch in guns. Any time the pilot selects the weapon in the air-to-air mode the central computer automatically commands the proper radar parameters and HUD and radar displays. Missile sequencing and prelaunch preparation, or tuning, are taken care of automatically. In addition the gun can be fired at any time the master arm switch is on.

A digital readout tells the pilot how many of the 940 rounds of 20mm ammunition remain in the gun – this is repeated on the HUD. The centre position on the weapon select switch brings to bear the AIM-9 Sidewinders carried on the inboard wing pylon. The priority and status of all onboard Sidewinders is displayed on the armament control panel. Selection of SRM (short range missile) commands the radar to

Right: View through the HUD with guns selected. The radar has the target designator box locked on an F-5E while the Eagle is flying at Mach 0.464 and pulling 4g. The vertical range indicator shows 34kts rate of closure. *MCAIR*

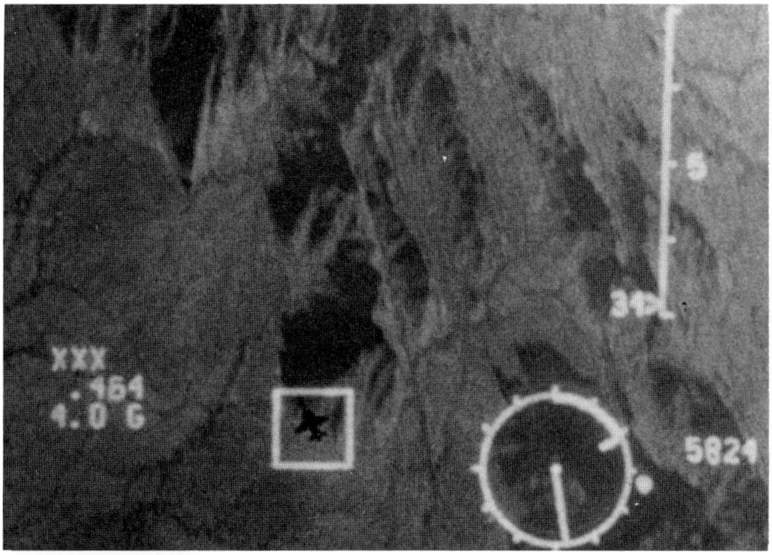

Below: HUD in the Short Range Missile (SRM or Sidewinder) mode. This places a circle in the target designator box. The F-15 is at 9,900ft (far right) at a calibrated airspeed of almost 550kts (far left) in a 60° left turn passing through 343° magnetic heading (top). The target is in range (IN RNG) with a relative speed of 564kts. *MCAIR*

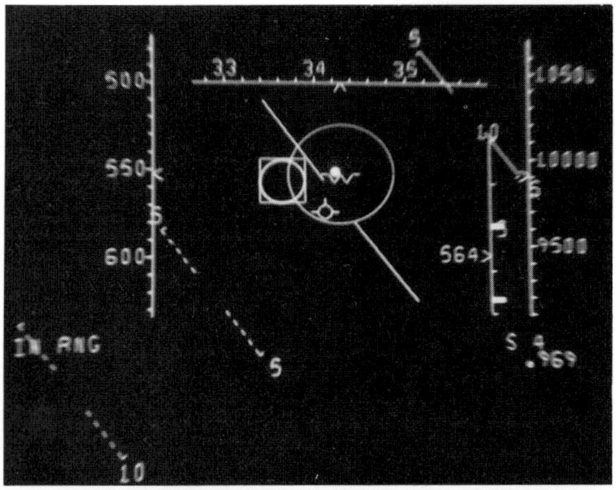

Bottom: This is what a SRM launch looks like on the radar scope (Air Navigation Multiple Indicator or ANMI). The display indicates the missile has been launched with 50sec until missile impact. *MCAIR*

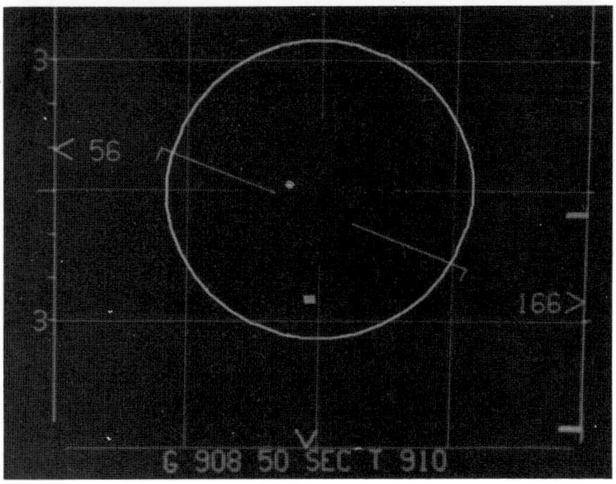

the 20-mile range and again lock on can be achieved automatically or manually with an off boresight capability. As in the guns mode there is no need to peek at the cockpit controls – the HUD displays all essential information. Also as in guns mode, the gun cross indicates the master arm is on. The number of missiles on board is displayed and R max and R min (range) cues indicate an approximation to the missile's actual firing range limits. Range rate is digitally displayed adjacent to the range marker – the in-range cue (IN RNG) is displayed when the range cue appears between R max/R min. As with the guns mode, a target designation box appears with aim dot and seeker circle. When the pilot uncages the Sidewinder's seeker head, the ASE circle expands to indicate the seeker head field of view.

The AIM-7 Sparrow works in essentially the same manner but with the radar HUD displays in MRM (medium range missile). In normal operation the Sparrows are automatically tuned when the radar is turned on. Within two minutes the Sparrows tune as the armament control set receives a tune signal and then a standby on the armament panel. If certain missiles are 'broken' (or malfunctioning) then they are eliminated from the firing sequence by the control computer. From that point on any time MRM is selected and the master arm is tuned on, a 'ready' cue will be displayed on the armament panel for each tuned MRM. Firing the radar missile, of course, requires head-down work to find the radar blip and lock-on. After this, necessary steering and/or status information is available on the HUD.

When in range, depressing the pickle button fires one MRM. The HUD then displays missile time of flight as a cue to the pilot to maintain radar lock-on for that period of time.

As far as the air-to-air weapons themselves the Sparrows are mounted externally on the aircraft not to prejudice any of the internal capacity or capability, while the heat-seeking Sidewinders are placed on pylons under the wings.

Currently pilots are still doubtful of the Sparrow's capabilities even though the radar has far reaching eyes and excellent capability. The missile itself, in Vietnam and since, has proven to be quite disappointing in its ability first of all to fire (it takes quite some time to ready itself) and when fired actually to track and kill the target. The pilots have been much happier with the short range Sidewinder and guns and consider the F-15 to be optimally faced with a close-in dogfight rather than a stand-off war.

There is no doubt that the Hughes AN/APG-63 radar in the Eagle is the most sophisticated of its kind in launching radar guided Sparrow missiles, Sidewinder heat seekers, or firing the 20mm cannon. The output of this X-band pulse doppler system is presented on a television-type scanned display (the VSD) rather than a cathode ray tube. The TV-type display is 'clean' which means that it presents no 'noisy' radar outputs. Instead, it displays only artificial blips where the signal-processing computer thinks it sees a target. This eliminates much radar scope interpretation, making the process feasible for a single seat aircraft. On the other hand, it means that the display makes it difficult to recognise simple jamming or multiple manoeuvring targets. The high pulse repetition frequency (PRF) normally employed in air interception radar does well in detecting targets at long range approaching from the front when the closing speeds are quite great. Yet in tail chases or other situations where the target is moving away from the attacking aircraft and is seen against ground clutter, high PRF transmissions are not satisfactory and a lower frequency for the pulse trains is preferred.

Arranging for the two sets of frequencies to be generated, transmitted and processed simultaneously in one unit has been the primary achievement of the radar. According to many analysts the successful combination of high and medium PRFs was undoubtedly the main reason for Hughes' victory over Westinghouse for the radar contract with McDonnell.

The dish scans to about 150 miles optimally within a volume of 60° on either side of the aircraft centre line and plus or minus 10° in pitch in the primary search mode. The radar is also able to interrogate IFF returns to determine which aircraft are friendly and which are not. This is all well and good if everyone's IFF equipment is working, or there is no jamming, but the problem in actual combat comes when this kind of equipment fails and beyond visual range the radar will not tell who is friendly and who is not.* Fighter pilots continue to insist that the dictum of 'he who sees first lives' still holds true because pilots will be forced to put their eyes on the target, visually

*Non Cooperative Target Recognition (NCTR) gear to differentiate between friendly and hostile radar is being investigated to solve the problem, although researchers are quick to point out the solution may not be found soon.

Left: The heart of the Eagle's beyond visual range capabilities – the Hughes AN/APG-63 radar and its associated black boxes. *MCAIR*

Right: Three F-15As in early 1976 just before joining the 1st Wing at Langley AFB, Virginia. *USAF*

Right: Various external stores attached to F-15s for air-to-ground evaluation, January and February 1974. *MCAIR*

identify it as friendly or enemy and react accordingly. The only exception to this might be in a Warsaw Pact scenario when an initial attack is launched and everyone realised that all the aircraft on one side of the border are enemy and all the aircraft on the other side of the border are not. Then the first firing pass can be made beyond visual range. But once the aircraft pass each other and begin to fight at extended and close-in ranges, it's going to be a matter of sorting out things with the eyeballs. This problem is discussed in some detail in Chapter 7.

The aircraft is all digital, a major breakthrough, and this has simplified maintenance as well as ease of interpretation in using the system. The aircraft is scheduled for a Tactical Electronic Warfare System (TEWS), an internally integrated electronic countermeasure (ECM) system, which can detect an enemy threat and then give the pilot options to defeat that threat. The system comprises a radar warning receiver, tail warning set, interference blanker, internal countermeasure set and flare/chaff dispenser. Most of it works automatically, allowing the pilot to attend to other chores in the cockpit.

With as many complex avionics as there are, the aircraft has another system that monitors everything and then isolates a failure so that the pilot can tell maintenance personnel what the problem is. This is known as the built-in test (BIT) which is implemented by line replaceable units (LRUs). The system is innovative in that the maintenance personnel yank a box out and replace it with another. But as mentioned in discussing the 1st Wing's workup to combat readiness, the problem was the ground equipment on base that has to work with the aircraft's black boxes and not the airborne equipment itself that ended up grounding many aircraft.

The system is available for the air-to-ground attack role as well since all three pylons on the inboard wing stations and centreline can carry up to 5,100lb making each station compatible with a typical load of six 500lb bombs carried on multiple ejector racks (MERs). Each wing also has an outboard station with a 1,300lb capacity for carrying ECM pods or other ordnance loads. The very strengths that make the F-15 a good air-to-air fighter make it a good air-to-ground fighter since it is designed for a negative 3g or positive 7.33g and has high energy manoeuvrability. All the Sparrow and Sidewinder missiles can be carried on the aircraft without compromising the bomb load.

With a full internal fuel load and one centreline tank, the F-15 was designed to carry six bombs on each wing station. The F-4 can carry only three bombs on each wing pylon and six on the centreline.

McDonnell Douglas' reasoning behind converting the Eagle to the attack role takes into account the advent of multi-threat defense systems facing attack aircraft which will be required to carry their bombs through surface-to-air missiles, anti-aircraft fire and enemy aircraft in order to reach the target and return home. Not too much can be said about how the aircraft might fly and handle with air-to-ground loads since stores clearance tests and air-to-ground operational tests ceased with the USAF decision to limit the F-15 to air-to-air. Despite USAF statements that the Eagle has 'not a pound for air-to-ground'

abroad, it has incorporated a great deal of electronics for the air-to-ground mission.

One of these electronic subsystems is a digital dive bombing system with features similar to those of the A-7. The system has a highly automated approach to weapon management, attack mode selection and weapon delivery. Through digital interfaces, it automatically controls the HUD presentation, radar antenna positioning, radar mode selection and weapon release computations.

The F-15's MER-200 bomb racks can also sustain a load factor of 7.33g compared with the 5g for most bomb racks. This may give the pilot a bit more manoeuvrability to play with during weapons delivery roll-in or pull-out.

There is also a radar ground mapping mode for course navigation and if necessary, for radar offset

Overleaf:

Top left: The 'Streak Eagle' taxies in at Grand Forks AFB, ND, after one of its record breaking time-to-climb records in January 1975. Note the full pressure suit the pilot is wearing. *USAF*

Bottom left: Eagles from the 1st Wing at Langley AFB join A-7s from Davis-Monthan AFB, Canadian F-104s and other Allied Aircraft from Maple Flag at Cold Lake, Canada – 11 May 1978. *USAF*

Top right: Two Eagles from the 36th Wing at Bitburg, Germany head out on a practice sortie. *USAF*

Bottom right: January 1975 – the F-15 'Streak Eagle' approaches Grand Forks AFB, North Dakota after breaking one of the world time-to-climb records. *USAF*

STREAK EAGLE

FF
AF 75 0025

USAF

Above : Air-to-ground evaluation trials for external stores, January/February 1974. *MCAIR*

bombing. However, the system does not lend itself well to radar bombing because the synthetic display on the VSD does not match the well-defined detail of a cathode ray tube.

The inertial navigation set detects aircraft motion and converts it to velocity, altitude and position change, providing the pilot with, among other things, the means of selecting one of 12 possible memorised destinations, or one of three targets of opportunity which can be inserted at will. It is, of course, not accurate enough for use in determining bomb release points.

On the HUD the target designator box performs the same function that it does in air-to-air, that is the pilot can see the selected airborne or ground target when it comes into visual range by looking through the box within the one or more mile inaccuracy of the INS.

The F-15 weapons delivery system provides five different modes of bomb delivery. Automatic and continuously displayed impact modes, as with the A-7, provide computed ballistics that don't limit the pilot to specific delivery parameters. The auto mode is more suitable for bombing missions to heavily defended areas where there is a desire to preserve some accuracy while releasing from inherently less accurate high release altitudes. In theory, this mode allows the pilot to continue to manoeuvre his aircraft until just prior to bomb release, but in practice with the A-7, these manoeuvres degrade accuracy.

The CDIP (Continuously Displayed Impact Point) mode might be used on close air support missions because the pilot controls the release of the bomb. It is more accurate at lower dive angles than the auto mode.

In the auto and CDIP modes, another feature similar to the A-7 allows the HUD to display a pull-up cue that tells the pilot when he must initiate a recovery to avoid bomb fragmentation or to miss the ground.

The guided weapon mode is used to deliver electro-optical or infra-red weapons. The HUD's reticle is slaved to the weapon's seeker head so that the pilot need only put the reticle aiming dot on the target, uncage the seeker head and release the bomb. On electro-optical bomb deliveries the ANMI (air navigation multiple indicator or the VSD scope in the air-to-ground mode) also displays seeker head video. Laser guided weapons are delivered in the same manner as conventional bombs using auto, CDIP or direct modes.

The direct mode is considered a backup means of delivery when the previous modes have failed. For an accurate delivery, preplanned dive-angle, airspeed, release altitude and 'g'-loading must be met as the depressed reticle aiming dot passes through the target. Included on the reticle is a slant range bar that may increase bombing accuracy over terrain of unknown elevation.

The manual mode is used when the rest of the weapon delivery system has malfunctioned. A manually depressed reticle is the only symbol displayed on the HUD.

As a side point to the capability of the target designator box to find the target, selecting a target on the INS panel calls up information (latitude, longtitude, altitude) that was previously stored in the

INS. This causes the target designator to be displayed on the HUD at the computed position of the target. In addition to the HUD display, the HSI (Horizontal Situation Indicator) also presents computed distance and bearing, magnetic heading and command heading information. When the pilot designates the target, he is telling the central computer where the target is with respect to the aircraft. Then the pilot can utilise the following means to find the target. (1) He may fly over a known identification point and insert known offset distances to the target; (2) He can visually acquire the target and place the HUD's target designator over the target; (3) He can slave the target designator to the reticle aiming dot and manoeuvre the aircraft so as to place the aiming dot on the target; (4) Designation can also be accomplished using the radar ground map mode and placing the cursor over the target.

One big plus as far as the F-15's survivability – it is one of the few fighter aircraft with a fire extinguishing system which is available for either engine or the accessory drive unit. The oxygen system has been isolated in a sealed compartment to increase fire protection further. The fuel system has been filled with reticulated foam, a weight and volume penalty, so that all internal fuel tanks are guarded against fires or explosions. All feed tanks are self-sealing for protection from up to .50 calibre bullets, fuel lines are routed through fuel tanks whenever possible and fuel lines outside of the tanks are covered with a self-sealing material. All internal fuel tanks are located forward of the engine and in a separate compartment, but they are adjacent to the inlets – a shot into the fuel can cause a leak into the inlet.

The Eagle also has three hydraulic systems that are powered by four hydraulic pumps. Any one of the three systems will provide adequate power for flight control and each hydraulic system is capable of detecting any loss of hydraulic fluid from one of its subsystems, then isolating that subsystem so the entire system will not be lost.

The electrical system is composed of two AC generators, two DC transformer rectifiers and one hydraulically powered emergency AC generator for critical aircraft systems.

The Eagle's flight control system has many features to improve survivability. Only one of the two vertical stabilisers is required to maintain directional control. Aileron and stabilator controls have safety spring cartridges that allow operation of a single aileron-stabilator combination if the other side should become jammed. If both ailerons become jammed, the differential stabilators will provide lateral control for moderate flight manoeuvres including landing. If all mechanical flight control linkages are severed, the F-15 will operate on the Control Augmentation System for return to base.

Air Force experience in the past regarding maintenance has been an ever-increasing trend of MMH/FH because of ever-increasing complexity. In other words, it required a great deal more ground time to get an airplane to fly one hour, reaching its pinnacle so far in the F-111 which requires close to 50 MMH/FH. Compare this to the 8 MMH/FH for the P-51 back in 1944 or 16 for the F-5A in 1965.

The F-15's designers spent a great deal of time with maintenance support particularly in view of the complexity of the on-board systems. The design specification required a figure for maintenance close to that of the P-51 with an estimate somewhere around 8 MMH/FH. By the time the F-15's category testing was complete, the figure had come down to only 19 MMH/FH, not quite as good as the F-5, but certainly better than the F-4E. By 1979, however, MMH/FH were up to 35 or about the same as the F-4. Operational readiness was at 56%, costing $4,300 per flight hour.

The Eagle had to fit into the USAF system for (1) organisational (flight line 'on aircraft' squadron maintenance) (2) intermediate (hangar and in shop 'off aircraft' maintenance at the base); and (3) depot (specialised repair and overhaul performed at separate facility) maintenance.

The F-15 was proving reliable at organisational level, passing complex maintenance problems up to the intermediate and depot levels. As described in Chapter 3, problems began to arise with support equipment for the aircraft. Avionics repair and support equipment, shortages of parts and engine problems ended up interferring drastically so that the MMH/FH figure was climbing. This took place at the intermediate and depot levels of maintenance due to

Overleaf:

Top left: This view of an F-15A in January 1976 gives a good look at its standard 'Compass Ghost' grey camouflage scheme. *USAF*

Bottom left: March 1978 – an F-15A of the 1st TFW banks over the flight line at Langley AFB, Virginia. Note that it is fully armed with AIM-9 Sidewinders and AIM-7 Sparrows. *USAF*

Top right: During 'Arctic Express', 17 February-12 March 1978, F-15s from the 36th Wing at Bitburg, Germany took part in a multi-national combat readiness exercise in arctic weather. This three-ship formation is over mountains on the coast of Norway. *USAF*

Bottom right: Another view of F-15s taken during 'Arctic Express' in March 1978. *USAF*

100

FF
032

BT
035
BT
063
BT
045

maximum use of highly automated test equipment being an integral part of how the concept would work. The equipment proved to be not up to standard and in some ways not very realistic. The idea was to facilitate rapid analysis of failures and quick replacement of failed modules and parts. Many of the LRUs (Line Replacement Units) ended up being difficult to repair, until there were no more LRUs in stock to put back in the aircraft.

Another goal was fewer personnel required to work on the aircraft since the automated test equipment would be doing most of the work. Again, as the 1st Wing found out at Langley getting the aircraft into operational readiness, this was not becoming the reality they had hoped.

There was another factor involved in that direct MMH/FH presented did not include ASE, munitions, precision measurement equipment laboratory, training equipment of general support maintenance, all of which required more people or higher skills from previous aircraft.

The aircraft is accessible with 570sq ft of access doors and panels, 67 doors consisting of 283sq ft with accessibility via quick release fasteners. This compares to 55sq ft on the F-4E, or 515% greater. 85% of the doors and panels are accessible without workstands. Radome avionic access doors and armament doors contain built in jury struts to retain the doors open safely in a high wind. The only time the radome has to be opened is for maintenance on the antenna drive. All other radar LRUs are located under quick release doors. This is somewhat similar to the F-111.

All servicing or servicing verification is accomplished through quick release doors located within larger quick release panels to reduce access time during preflight, turn around and post flight. Main hydraulic ground power connections can be made through the wheel wells. The utility hydraulic system connects through a quick release door. Refuelling is also accomplished through a quick release door without need of electrical power. The following are R&D test figures on fast-servicing the aircraft:

Oil check	1 minute
Internal fuelling	5 minutes
Internal plus external fuelling	7 minutes
Engine Oil Service	4 minutes
Complete Aircraft Lubrication	4 hours, 15 minutes/ manhours

All previous Century series fighters have required drag chutes which require considerable servicing, happily the F-15 has no drag chute.

Some thinking went into how the aircraft would be serviced simultaneously from many different areas. All hydraulic ground power connections, electrical power connections, ground cooling connections and general servicing connections are well separated to permit simultaneous maintenance without interference between equipment or congestion of work areas. The LOX (liquid oxygen) convertor is located well clear of potential fire/explosion sources, permitting quick LOX change, even while refuelling or rearming.

Below: The F-15 is an accessible airplane with 570sq ft of openable area, 85% of which can be reached without stands. *MCAIR*

Rearming can be accomplished quickly, as with other aircraft. For one thing, as noted before, the armament controls and monitors are consolidated into a single panel. Ammunition can be reloaded rapidly and the cleaning cycle for the MER-200s is every 15 shots. Launchers are interchangeable from left to right and front to rear. Wing pylons are interchangeable between any station. Gun system component separation permits replacement of either the gun, gun drive, or ammunition storage container without need to down load the entire system as would be the case with palatised equipment.

In a 'no maintenance' air superiority configuration without Sidewinders, R&D tests found the F-15 can be turned around in 12 minutes while loading four AIM-7Fs, 940 rounds of 20mm ammunition and servicing fuel and LOX. The MER-200, which was designed for the F-15, has a 33% better remove and replace time over the MER-10 used on the F-4E and an 80% improved cleaning cycle over the F-4E. After the gun is replaced, assuming it has to be, it requires no bore sighting, which again is a step forward.

Both McDonnell Douglas and the Air Force hope to solve the recurring problems in the F-15s fault isolation system. This is how F-15 fault isolation is supposed to work: first, the caution light panel in the cockpit goes on, warning of in-flight failure. Second, the built-in test (BIT) control panel, also in the cockpit, is used for ground test and in-flight system assessment. Third, the avionic status panel in the nose wheel isolates the fault to an area or an LRU. And fourth, an LRU fail flag in the avionics space specifies the piece of equipment that is haywire. Then the maintenance technician can open the panels and get to the equipment quickly.

As in previous aircraft, avionic equipment is functionally grouped. That is, bay number one left contains the F-15 radar set. Bay number one right contains C&I and navigational equipment, and so on.

The emphasis throughout is modular construction so everything can be pulled out, tested and replaced. This includes printed circuit boards, alignment guides, captive screws, and other such refinements. Self-locking swing bolts are also incorporated which means a positive lock; no safety wire, no foreign object damage, and no tools.

The Eagle is also crammed with failure cues/indicators and sight gauges for including such things as the engine event history recorder, gear box sight gauge, ECS valve position indicator, engine oil sight gauge, central gear box sight gauge, main landing gear brake wear indicator (a unique little pin that descends as the brake wears), landing gear strut pressure gauge, hydraulic accumulator volume indicator, and so on.

The wiring harnesses are smaller, now referred to as micromini. When compared to the conventional harness of 1959 which weighed 24.81lb, there is quite a change as reduced to 9.6lb now. No potting or solder is used in the system either.

The fuel system has a fuel ground check panel, a two-latched hinged quick access door, located near the ground refuelling receptacle which pops out, providing a full panel for refuelling the aircraft. While standing there a maintenance technician can trouble shoot the entire fuel system, and it permits transfer of fuel to any tank both internal and external. The self-sealing fuel lines have seals at all flex joints, attaching to the engine with a self-locking quick disconnect. No tools are required for connecting or disconnecting the lines.

Hydraulics maintenance has been eased by large quick access doors that are hinged. There are no accumulators required in any of the basic systems. Two filters each for PC-1 and PC-2 and three filters for the utility system are required. The filter elements are interchangeable with any other filter element in any of the three hydraulic systems. There are built in safety locks on all filter bowls which eliminate safety wire/cotter pins. A mechanic can hand tighten the bowl since no torque wrench or tools are required for removal or installation of any filter bowl.

The landing gear has some maintenance-reducing features as well. There are carbon brakes which are 70lb lighter than the F-4E and the brakes can be assembled as a unit, stuck on or taken off. The brake anti-skid has a built-in test and the single axle nut permits replacement of the wheel/tyre assembly in five minutes. The strut design incorporates seal replacement without strut removal.

The airframe in general has interchangeable parts and a simple wing. A wing change is supposed to be made at the intermediate level with eight hours elapsed time and without special skills.

Overleaf:

Top left: November 1977 – A 1st Tactical Fighter Wing F-15A off the coast of North Carolina with a centreline auxiliary fuel tank. *USAF*

Bottom left: During 'Ready Holloman' the 18th TFW at Holloman AFB began to receive Eagles to replace ageing F-4s. Here two new 49th F-15As hold position off a KC-135 as a 461st Squadron, 58th Tactical Training Wing F-15B takes on fuel, March 1978. *USAF*

Top and bottom right: Col Perry Smith in an F-15A over the North Sea. Smith was CO of the 36th TFW at the time of the author's flight. *Author*

FF
AF 76 054

HO
HO
AF 76 068
U.S. AIR FORCE
LA

BT
072

5. The Engine

The F-15 has such good manoeuvring performance because of its wing and its engine. Any fighter performance advance depends primarily on advances in propulsion, specifically in thrust-to-weight ratio.

The F100 evolved from a competition with an engine designed by General Electric. Its development is credited by its designers and engineers to a steady evolution of design application, selection of materials and accelerated testing. When the original Request For Proposal (RFP) was issued in April of 1968, Pratt & Whitney had been involved in production engines such as the TF30-P-1, which was to be installed in the F-111; the TF30-P-412, used in the F-14A; and the J58 used in the SR-71. All three of these engines were significant steps forward.

An augmented turbofan engine in the 23,820lb thrust class, the F100 produces 25% more thrust per pound than P&WA's previous engines – weighing a little more than 3,000lb, it produces slightly less than 8lb of thrust for every pound of its weight, or about the same thrust-to-weight ratio as the 1968 J85-21. The F100, of course, has significantly better cruise fuel consumption than the J85.

In technical terms, the F100 is an axial-flow, low bypass, high compression ratio, twin spool engine with an annular combustor, electronic ignition, a common flow five-segment augmentor (afterburner) and a light weight balance beam nozzle. It has a three-stage fan and 10 stage compressor, each driven by its own turbine. Overall compression ratio is 23:1; bypass ratio is 0.72; and turbine temperature is 2,500°. This highly complex engine has certainly pushed temperature and pressure limits, as reflected in the $2million per engine total programme cost.

In explaining the engine's features Pratt & Whitney's designers point to the high aerodynamic stage loadings, a high temperature turbine with advanced cooling techniques, the use of high strength, low weight alloys and a balanced beam exhaust nozzle. The engine is also modularly constructed so that major parts or sections can be removed for maintenance while leaving most of the engine intact. One of the major design requirements intended to give the engine an edge in air-to-air combat was smoke prevention. The requirement was originally met. With recent engine adjustment to counter the stall/stagnation problem, however, smoke generation has been one unwelcome result.

The Government Products Division of the Pratt & Whitney Aircraft Group at West Palm Beach, Florida is the home of the F100. The Chief of F100 development attributes much of the engine's performace to the use of higher compressor-stage loadings. The F100 has five main shaft bearings, three for the low speed rotor and two for the high. Fewer stages and a shorter combustor produced the reduced shaft links that permit use of fewer bearings. The improved compressor and combustor technology results in a cumulative weight reduction. The shorter annular combustor with 16 fuel nozzles has some inherent advantages: the rotor shafts and ducts are shorter, thus saving in weight and simplifying critical speed problems. As a result of the engine being shorter, it is stiff, therefore less prone to flexing. P&WA's engineers were also able to increase turbine temperature in the engine by flowing cooling air through hollow blades and vanes of the first stage of the core turbine. The principle was nothing new – it had been done during World War 2 in the Jumo 004 of the Me262. Therefore blade metal temperature is reduced to approximately 1,800°F from 2,500°F at the blade surface. Employing electronics to fine-tune the engine, the Engine Electronics Control (EEC) monitors and trims the hydromechanical unified fuel control (UFC) to obtain the best fuel-to-air ratio.

The low weight of the engine resulted from the extensive use of tough lightweight materials – of its 3,020lb approximately 30% of the F100 is titanium alloy.

In talking with the engine's designers, it is clear they are particularly proud of the F100's balanced-beam exhaust nozzle which they feel is one of the most advanced elements of the engine. A convergent/divergent system, it is designed to get the most efficiency out of the engine at both supersonic and subsonic speeds. Each convergent flap operates

Right: This is what the F100 looks like at the Pratt & Whitney Aircraft plant in West Palm Beach, Florida. In the 24,000lb thrust class, this turbofan also powers the F-16 and was slated for the F-14B. *P&WA*

FF 056
FF 060
FF 091
FF 054

about a pivot. Forward ends are hinged to a balanced flap. In turn the flap is hinged at its forward end to a static structure. Gas loads are balanced; the outward gas loads on the balanced flap and the part forward on the convergent flap pivot counter balance the loads on the remainder of the convergent flap and on the divergent flap. This balanced-beam design permits yet another reduction in weight as compared to the conventional cantilever design.

The F100 is the first US fighter engine built for modular maintenance, another major design change. The engine is built in five major modules; fan, core (compressor, combustor/compressor-drive turbine), fan-drive turbine, augmentor, and gearbox. The great thing for the crew chief is that each module is interchangeable from engine to engine at the intermediate maintenance level. This means, theoretically, a whole engine isn't put out of action when repairs are needed. Thus, the number of spares required should be reduced.

As of 1979 maximum operating time for all modules was up to 1,250 hours. One of the major goals of the F100 programme is to perform maintenance only as required with no limitation on maximum operating hours, a maintenance concept that has been used by commercial airlines for over ten years.

Much of the engine performance has been seen in the accelerated mission test (AMT) being used by Pratt & Whitney. The AMT consists of four phases: (1) determing the actual mission profile; (2) defining test conditions; (3) AMT verification; (4) implementing required changes.

The AMT tailored to the F-15 was a 2,000-hour test. An analysis indicated that operation at idle and cruise power conditions had an insignificant impact on engine life. Therefore, only those things hardest on the engine – full throttle, high temperature time, and cold start take-offs – were included in the AMT.

In that 2,000 hours of use, the engine was specified to sustain a transient cycle from idle to sea level maximum power and back to idle 1,765 times (below 73% power to above 89% power). As a precuation, P&WA designed in an ability to go through 7,060 transient cycles in 2,000 hours.

What no one foresaw was an excess of power that forced pilots to continually reduce from military power to slow down during dogfights – that is just what happened to both the F-15 and F-16. By the summer of 1979, pilots in Europe were averaging over

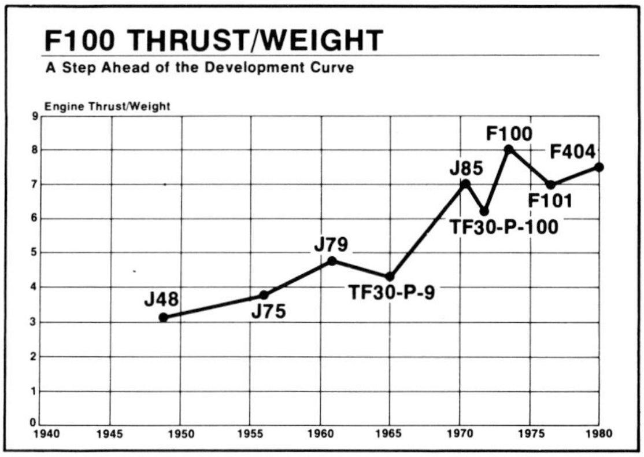

Above: F100 thrust to weight development curve. *P&WA*

Right: F100 was designed for modular construction and maintenance. *MCAIR*

Left: 21 November 1977 – a four-ship flight from Langley AFB (1st TFW) over Kitty Hawk, North Carolina, the birthplace of aviation. *USAF*

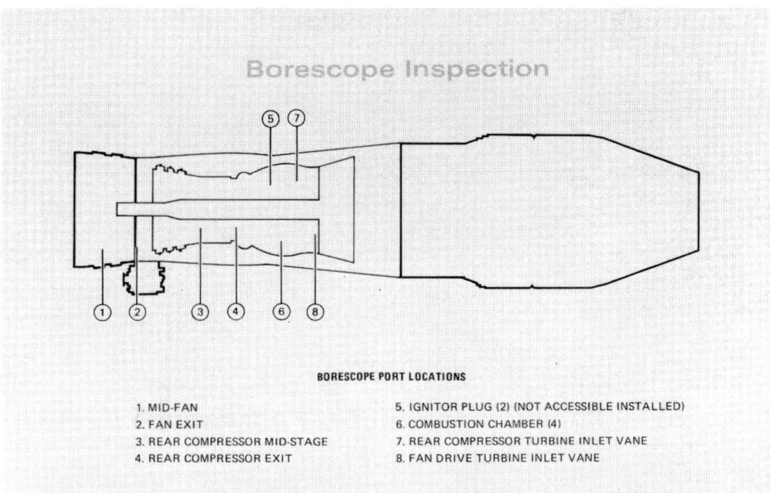

The F100 design facilitates the on-condition maintenance concept by providing borescope ports for inspection as illustrated, chip detectors, and built-in failure indicators.

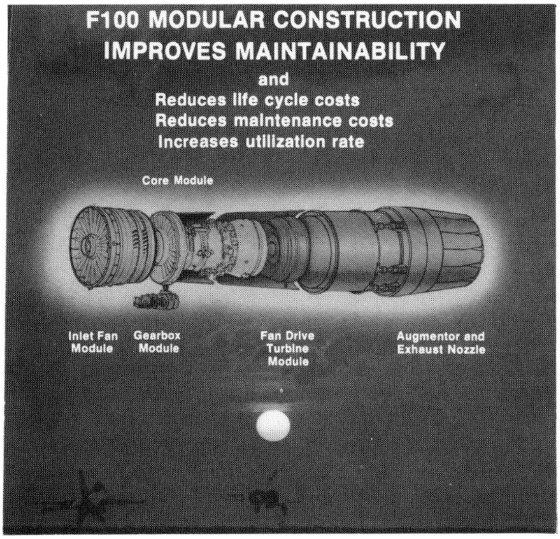

25,000 cycles in 2,000 hours of engine time. In addition, the excess thrust, due to changes in temperature during a dogfight, has reduced the lifetime of the turbine blades.

Undersecretary for Research and Engineering Dr William Perry, in responding to Congressional frustration over recurring engine problems noted, '. . our insistance on getting maximum performance from pushing the state of the art on the engine within the DoD is one of the culprits. And I think in that respect, we probably differ from the Soviets who are more inclined to accept what they get, and probably have a greater emphasis on maintainability than on getting the last 10% in thrust out of the engines.'

The engine endurance qualification test was the only milestone that the F-15 failed to meet on time.

Most of the publicity on the engine and its problems has been devoted to stall/stagnation. A stagnation occurs when a compressor stall degenerates into a condition from which the engine cannot be re-accelerated without first being shut down and then restarted. The engine winds down to a low thrust, low RPM state and will not answer to increases in throttle setting. It will overheat catastrophically if not shut down. Even though stagnations can take place anywhere in the flight envelope they tend to cluster toward the upper left corner at high altitudes and low speed. This problem has occurred on the ground, on take-off, in traffic patterns, and during air combat manoeuvres. Stalls can be initiated by rapid throttle movement, high angle of attack manoeuvres or 'hard' afterburner lights. In other words, any pressure disturbance in the inlet or afterburner can initiate a stall. And stalls, even when they don't stagnate, cause major decreases in engine life through transient overtemperatures.

There have been some other problems that P&WA has had to work on as well concerning the engine, including turbine blade integrity. Turbine blades have been lost due to 30% overspeed and 200°F over-temperature conditions due to stall/stagnations. The higher speeds impose greater centrifugal stresses on the blades, the yield strengths of which are reduced by the higher temperatures.

As of January 1979, the F-15 had accumulated 135,000 flying hours and nine losses or a loss rate of 6.6 per 100,000 flight hours. Engineers say they have reduced the rate of stall stagnation from its initial 1.8 per 1,000 hours to 0.6 per 1,000 hours with some modifications, including a sensor control system in the EEC that reduces flow and opens the exhaust nozzle when the system senses a pending stall.

The unreliable afterburner light-off problem and the related stall problem have definitely influenced F-15 tactics: pilots have to be careful not to move the throttles much while manoeuvring hard. Further, they tend to stay in burner once they have lit it. This, in turn, aggravates the F-15's inherently low fuel fraction and makes it easy to run out of fuel in a fight, as was particularly noticeable during the AIMVAL/ACEVAL tests (see Chapter 7).

Since the F100 powers both the F-15 and the F-16 it will be around for awhile. Pratt & Whitney engineers are already looking into future growth and derivatives of the engine, including the F100 Derivative II, that would bring increased durability, reduced maintenance, increased thrust and reduced parts. They are also looking into tailored nozzle systems, non-augmented engines and higher bypass ratios for transport use.

By the spring of 1979 there were 1,100 F100 engines in the inventory with plans to buy over 4,000 with a present maturation process historically narrowed down to about a 15-year length of time. Since many of the problems concern the F100 engine, it is only fair to point out in June of 1971 Pratt & Whitney Aircraft wrote a letter to the Joint Engine Project Office at Wright-Patterson AFB asking that the F100/F401 programme be subjected to a B-45 flying test bed so that the engine could be tested in the air before it was installed in the aircraft. There had been much discussion on the need to test fly the engine before it was put in the F-15. P&WA, at that time, said 'We believe very strongly that the availability of such a vehicle for the investigation and correction of flight associated problems is imperative to the timely operational suitability and readiness of the F-14B and F-15 weapons system.' They had done this on their previous engines that were of any major

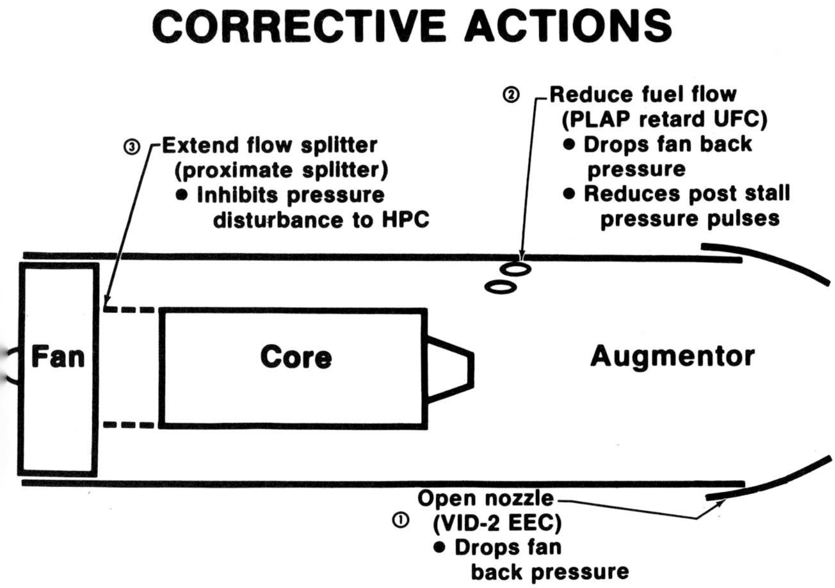

Left: Here is what Pratt & Whitney was doing in 1980 to correct problems in the F100. The 3 fix is for the F-16 only. *P&WA*

consequence, however the JEPO answered by saying, 'The increased engine testing hours and the lower cost by not utilising the B-45 are considered dominating factors . . . (Therefore) the test bed is considered inappropriate.'

It is ironic that the tests would have taken place on the B-45 in the upper left hand portion of the engine envelope where most of the problems are currently centred.

In November 1979 General Alton D. Slay, Commander, Air Force Systems Command, presented his report to the Senate Armed Services Committee on the problems with the F100 engine. As of that time 1,385 F100 operational engines had been delivered and the engine had met Air Force requirements in each of the three key performance parameters that were set for it: thrust, weight and specific fuel consumption. But he reported it had not met their needs for durability nor for ease of maintenance.

As of General Slay's report there had been 755 stall/stagnations in the F-15 and none in the operational F-16 fleet which uses the same engine (though F-16s have since suffered from the problem).*

Attempted remedies for the phenomenon involved three specific engine modifications. The first was to change afterburner settings upon sensing a stall. The second was reducing afterburner fuel flow to minimum and opening the afterburner nozzle, thereby decreasing afterburner pressure pulses from sustaining a compressor stall. The changes were incorporated in all production engines and were being retrofitted during accessory depot maintenance.

The third remedy went into the F-16 engines, but because the USAF believed the F-15 had an extra safety margin with two engines, the modification cost convinced the Air Force that they should not incorporate it into the F-15. This remedy, the so-called proximate splitter, reduces the clearance between the fan exit and the structure which splits air flow between the compressor and the compressor bypass duct.

General Slay also made this comment in his report, 'We have experienced unanticipated durability problems which have lowered our fighter readiness, increased our need for spare engines and components and increased our engine maintenance work load in the field and depots. Our current engine shortfall ranges from 45 to 50 "below zero spares" which equates to "holes in aircraft" instead of "engines in aircraft." This is down from a high of 90 to 100 five months ago.'

Due to other factors the shortage was expected to increase instead of decrease. The most serious durability problem had been turbine failures, 54 as of November 1979. Thermal fatigue failures of the second stage turbine vane caused by over temperature during stall stagnation and by uneven temperature distribution in the combustor have been the principal causes.

Three stall/stagnation corrections were made, as mentioned previously, involving incorporation of newer technology material in the turbine vanes coming off the production line, and an engineering

*Since the stalls in the F-15 occur in the 13th stage of the compressor, versus the 7th stage in the F-16, the problem is more serious in the Eagle.

Right: The engine is accessible through several doors and it can be removed quickly, sliding out on rails. *MCAIR*

effort to correct the uneven combustor temperature profiles. Borescope inspection procedures initiated in March 1979 avoided some of the problem with the vanes, discovering and replacing the stressed vanes during 100-hour maintenance in the F-15. However, as General Slay pointed out, 'The inspections have all but eliminated turbine failure, but they have obviously aggravated an already severe logistic support problem and increased the maintenance support requirements. We clearly underestimated our logistic support requirements for the F100 engine. One major factor is that the historical measure of engine life – flight hours – was not the key measure. Our early estimates of engine life and hence, spare parts requirements, were based on engine removals per flight hour of the TF30 engine. We soon realised that this was wrong. We found engine life is closely related to the number of thermal cycles of mechanical stress loadings of the components. Again we erred on the low side. We based our revised spare parts requirement on a 1977 estimate of 1.5 cycles per engine flight hour, but found that we experienced 2.2 in the F-15 . . .

'This generated engine removals for maintenance faster than predicted. In addition, when we opened the engines to perform maintenance, we found greater component distress than we predicted. For instance, the condemnation rate for first stage turbine blades was not 20% as predicted – it was 60%. These problems combined to make spare parts usage much higher than anticipated.'

The Air Force began a series of actions to resolve this expensive problem. One was trimming the engines 80° lower. That is, reducing the engine's maximum gas temperature by 80°. They also reduced the engine run time required at maximum temperature to perform an engine trim from the original 22 minutes to 1 minute. And finally, the Air Force had to put a work force of contractor teams into the field to help because Air Force maintenance people were not able to handle the problems.

Slay made it clear that the other significant problems still had to be resolved. The initial underestimation of spare requirements gave the Air Force no margin for the problems experienced.

There was little capability to accelerate deliveries because parts replacement requires longer lead time, often from a limited number of sources. Added to that, two of Pratt & Whitney's manufacturing plants went on strike, a bearing manufacturer and a forging supplier, putting the programme even further behind in meeting F100 requirements. The engine production line slowdown resulted in a shortage of production engines, both for installation and spares, which at the time Slay estimated could result in as many as 43 F-15s and 53 F-16s without engines by the summer of 1980. P&WA hoped to recover from this strike by mid-1981, accelerating engine production by 75 engines in 1980.

In spite of how dismal all of this sounded, Slay made it clear that he believed the F-15 and F-16 were, beyond any doubt, two of the highest performing fighters in the world, if not *the* two highest performing fighters in the world. Slay attributed this in no small part to the impressive performance of the F100 engine. The second point he made was that he had

Right: Here is where all 47,640lb of thrust exits the Eagle as seen on this 57th TTW aircraft at Nellis. *USAF*

Below: TF-2 undergoes an engine change on 12 February 1974. *MCAIR*

never seen an operational jet fighter engine brought into the inventory without troubles. The General went on to say, 'I strongly believe that we must change our "way of life" in the engine development business. We need to learn and make use of several lessons from our experience with the F100 engine. We must design greater margin and greater tolerance into our engines. We must adjust our sights down from the performance extreme that we set on the F100 toward more durability in establishing our requirements. We must be sure we know that we are getting through a realistic and comprehensive test programme based on a conservative projection of how the engine will be used in operational service. We must develop and maintain necessary second sources for critical components. We must do our spares planning conservatively. Many spares have long lead times with limited capability for delivery acceleration.'

General Slay was also a strong proponent in developing an alternative fighter engine so that the industry could compete with itself in developing the best engines available while saving dollars. For this reason he desired to push for the development of the F101 derivative fighter engine, which had a good head start in the joint Air Force/Navy project. By 1981 it was flying in the F-16. General Slay made this final comment in his report: 'I strongly believe that future engine development must be initiated well ahead of the aircraft it will power. I have set my people on a course to that end. By starting engine development earlier, I think we can better ensure reliable, durable, higher performing and well developed engines for any new aircraft requirement that might arise.'

6. Into the Future

By April 1980 the Eagle programme had delivered 504 aircraft to the USAF and 25 to Israel (383 A models, 60 B models and 82 C models). There were orders for another 229 aircraft for the Air Force and eight to Japan in April 1981 ('Peace Eagle I') 15 to Israel, 60 to Saudi Arabia and another four to Japan in April-June 1983 under 'Peace Eagle II'. The Japanese are preparing to introduce another 120 or more Eagles to their inventory.

The F-15C and F-15D models, initial delivery to the Air Force starting in mid-1979, have several improvements, many of which are being retrofitted to the A and B models. The APG-63 radar of the C and D models has a high speed digital computer known as a programmable signal processor (PSP) to permit future software changes instead of hard wiring modifications. This amounts to replacing a tape that gives the system new instructions for meeting changed conditions.

The modification is expected to provide a four-fold increase in F-15 computer capacity, including the ability to continue tracking one target while searching for others and the ability to transfer radar lock-on from one target to another as in the F-14. Also planned for inclusion is a radar aid assessment mode, a feature intended to allow the radar to identify targets within a massed raid that normally looks like one radar return. With doppler beam sharpening there is improvement in the ability to separate multiple targets within the radar's beam width. The F-15 radar range is quite adequate in high PRF mode which doesn't see tail-on or crossing targets. The medium PRF mode is supposed to see both opening and closing targets and is therefore important for large air battles as in Europe. Unfortunately, the medium PRF mode is proving short ranged, failing to see a number of targets. In fact, F-15s and F-16s are sighting each other at the same time on their radars in Europe.

The new processor projects flight status and tracking information for each target. When it works, the pilot then knows if the enemy aircraft are climbing, diving or turning to avoid interception. It has a capacity to track up to eight targets while searching for other intruders. These tracking schemes can be defeated, however, by manoeuvring targets.

McDonnell Douglas has initiated also the Production Eagle Package or PEP-2000. This is a fuel increase to 13,455lb total internal, with the FAST packs that goes up to 10,000lb additional while the aircraft can still carry three external tanks. With the increase in weight, wheels, tyres and brakes had to be modified; performance also suffers.

The PSP evolved from the AIMVAL/ACEVAL programme of 1978 along with the possibility of improved missiles such as the AIM-7M + Sparrow which was to have electronic countermeasure capability and shoot down improvement, and the AIM-9L which was to be an all-aspect infra-red missile that could be fired at a target head-on.

However, there has been a great deal of discussion within the Air Force community about radar missiles themselves and their reliability (see Chapter 7).

One of the problems with the all-aspect infra-red missile was its extreme sensitivity – it would track on tiny heat sources such as a warm rock or even sparkling snow. Research is being directed at a seeker head that will differentiate between various heat sources to pick the proper target.

One interesting addition that has been showing up in F-15 cockpits is a x6 rifle telescope called 'Eagle Eye' mounted on the right or left side of the HUD matching the centreline of the aircraft.

F-15 pilots who were using the rifle scopes gained a significant advantage in their ID of bogey aircraft, so it could be showing up more and more as an unofficial modification or possibly later as an Air Force buy.

With the overseas buys of F-15s by Japan, Israel and Saudi Arabia, it is interesting to note that the aircraft in the Middle East in particular may be facing themselves, although at present there are no major rifts between the Saudis and the Israelis. (The Israelis did protest at the sale of the 60 F-15s to Saudia Arabia.)

American fighter pilots have not missed the significance of this possibility. With the weapons sales posture of the US, types of American manufacture may be facing each other, driving the requirements

Right: TF-2, the FAST Pack pallet prototype, shown here on 20 August 1974 before going to Farnborough the next month. *MCAIR*

for visual identification to the sublime. Not only will a pilot have to ascertain, for example, if the opposing aircraft is an F-14 or F-15, but he will have to get close enough to see the markings before taking appropriate action! This concern was expressed to the author by an F-14 squadron commander.

The Israelis are using their F-15s in every possible mission, carrying a wide range of payloads, including FAST packs. Israeli pilots also have not been greatly worried about much of the equipment on board working. In their combats with Syrian MiGs in 1979 (see Chapter 7), the Israelis found that the primary combat was close-in, hard manoeuvring, using heat seekers or guns. This negated a strong reliance on the radar and the beyond visual range concept. They found that the F-15 was highly capable in its air-to-air mission, but again, the lesson to be learned is that the dogfight is not an exercise of the past, but a very present capability to be maintained.

In December 1976 when the Japan Air Self Defence Force (JASDF) selected the F-15 as its next generation fighter, a two-year process was completed that had started with the following aircraft in consideration: the Viggen of Sweden; the Tornado developed jointly by the United Kingdom, West Germany and Italy; the Mirage F-1 of France; and the F-14, F-15, F-16 and F-17 of the United States. The aircraft that would eventually be selected was to equip ten of the 13 fighter squadrons of the JASDF. The F-104J units, in deployment since 1962, were scheduled to be deactivated completely by 1985, and even though the F-4EJ remains the mainstay of Japan's Air Forces, defence planners realised that a superior intercept aircraft would be required. By 1976 the candidates had been reduced to the F-14, F-15 and F-16, with procurement to be initiated in 1977 for 123 aircraft to equip the first five fighter squadrons. The new aircraft in consideration was primarily for intercept with a secondary ground support capability, depending on the circumstances.

Japan is an oblong group of islands that spans quite a distance with a wide range of both topography and weather. The new aircraft would have to operate in these conditions in such a way as to get to altitude rapidly and stop any incoming force. When the JASDF was formed, it was under the specific direction of the constitution that it never make an aggressive move. This means that any force facing Japan's aircraft would be met over the Japanese islands.

The F-15, according to Japan's planners, had an excellent climb and acceleration capability in comparison with the F-14 and this was to be of prime importance in making the final choice. Once up, the aircraft would have to spend some time in the air since

Below: McDonnell hopes to see the F-15 production line kept open with expanded use of the aircraft. This chart shows some of the possibilities. *MCAIR*

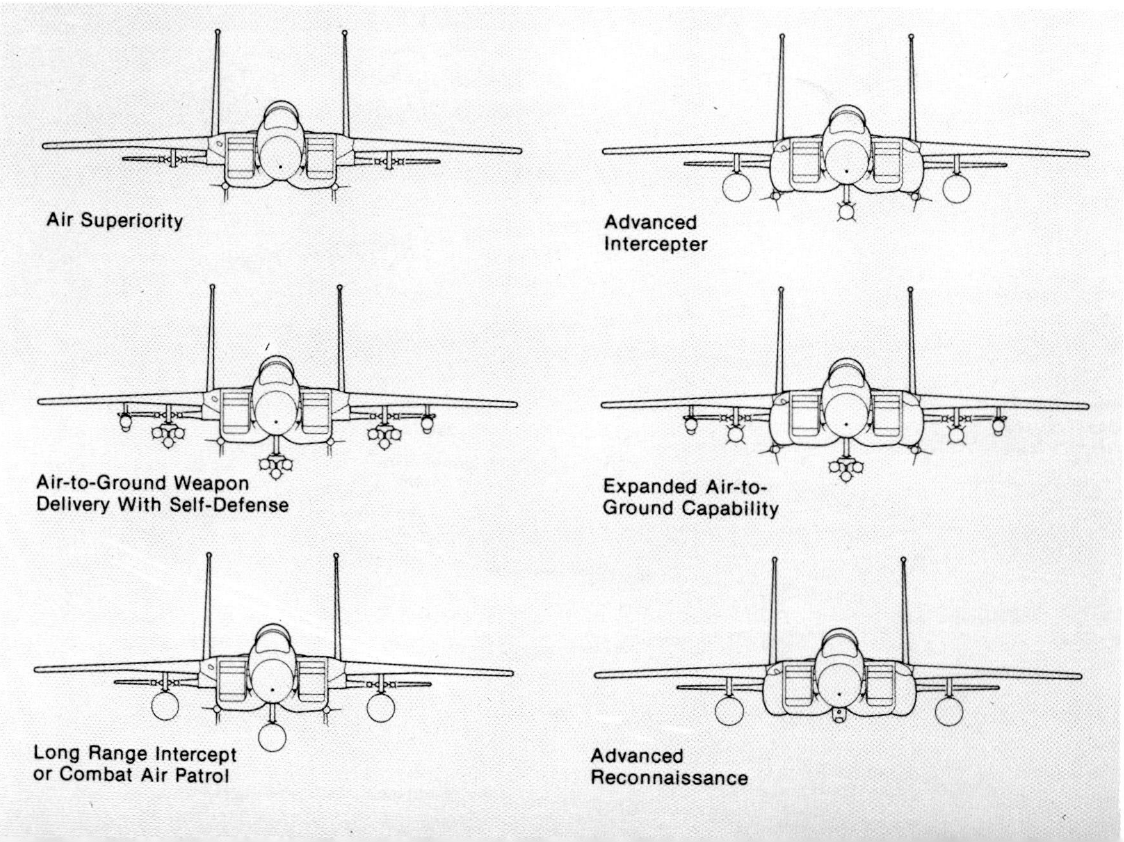

point defence was not the objective, but the entire defence of the island chain.

The following parameters were outlined for the final Japanese selection of the F-15: combat capability under all-weather conditions; capability against high altitude, high speed targets; capability against low altitude targets; air-to-air combat capability; electronics capability; capability to operate independently in the air; and finally safety, training reliability, maintainability, importation and logistical support.

The Eagle has an internal growth space for 56cu ft of avionics and another 900lb of fuel, along with 40% unused electrical capacity, 14% unused cooling capacity and 55% unused computer capability. The digital avionics facilitate programming software changes into the system.

All that space behind the pilot in the F-15A and F-15C is a significant area for expansion in the form of a multi-mission aft cockpit which would allow a weapons system operator to use the aircraft fire control and weapons systems effectively during high task loading missions. In the F-15B and F-15D this second seat is used primarily for training, but McDonnell's engineers, designers and planners have this second seat in mind for a number of additional systems.

McDonnell is pinning its hopes in keeping the aircraft on the production line with four basic building blocks: the FAST pack external pallets, the multi-mission aft cockpit, the PEP-2000 modification and the advanced radar with the new programmable signal processor and an expanded radar data processor. McDonnell sees the current F-15C with the following additions: additional radar modes, fuel/sensor FAST packs, JTIDS (Joint Tactical Information Distribution System), infra-red search and track, long range communications, and additional missile carriage (eight additional AIM-7F missiles). These basic air-to-air enhancements are predicated on the beyond visual range concept. McDonnell planners would also like to see the F-15D set aside for the reconnaissance mission with the following additions: multi-mission aft cockpit, additional radar modes, fuel/sensor FAST packs, video data recorder/playback, video data link, electro-optical sensor, LORAN/GPS navigation and JTIDS. In MCAIR's opinion this would allow the F-15 to become an all-weather, real time reconnaissance night or day aircraft, with some APG-63 modifications to provide a forward looking high resolution ground map moving target indications/tract and terrain following/terrain avoidance modes. The FAST packs would have installed in them advanced photo systems, side looking radar, TEREC (Tactical Electronic Reconnaissance) and advanced sensors for all-weather targeting during low altitude penetration. An integrated forward-looking infra-red/electro-optical sensor system could be installed internally for target recognition. This capability could

Left: February 1979 – The first F-15C off the St Louis production line, over the well known St Louis Arch. *MCAIR*

Above: The No 2 Eagle was still hard at work with NASA into the 1980s – note that the wingtips have not been raked or modified as with operational military aircraft. There is also a lack of ECM gear aboard and no gun or missiles, as befits a pure research aircraft. Here Space Shuttle thermal protection tiles are being tested up to 1.5 the dynamic pressure that the Shuttle will attain during launch. The tiles on the right wing simulate the Shuttle's leading edge while those on the left represent the tiles on the junction of the Orbiter's wing and fuselage. *NASA*

be added, according to MCAIR, without removing air-to-air or air-to-surface features so that the aircraft could be configured for field conversion from reconnaissance to strike to air superiority.

The F-15D has been slated for consideration by the USAF as an all-weather air-to-ground interdiction aircraft that resembles the reconnaissance F-15 configuration, again with FAST packs and a multi-mission aft cockpit. The main impediment to USAF adoption and funding of this aircraft has been the tremendous cost, probably amounting to $40million per aircraft when R&D is included. These costs could force the USAF to sacrifice three to five wings in total force structure to pay for the programme.

MCAIR is talking of equipping a version of the F-15 with five cruise missiles and modifying the radar for terrain following and ground mapping with an integrated forward-looking infra-red/electro-optical sensor system to provide target recognition and track for weapon guidance and delivery. JTIDS, LORAN/GPS naviagation and helmet mounted sights are a part of the package as well. Again, MCAIR advertises the capability without removing air-to-air features, with the aircraft capable of being converted at field level for reconnaissance and air superiority missions.

Yet another possibility for the F-15D is the Wild Weasel or defence suppression mission that would carry Shrike and standard anti-radiation missiles along with cluster bombs for SAM suppression. Again the idea is not to remove the existing air-to-air and air-to-surface features but to configure the aircraft so that it could be converted at field level.

The F-15D has been suggested for tactical jamming system role, a mission to degrade hostile air defences by employing ECM against air surveillance acquisition and fire control radars. With a multi-mission aft cockpit, the F-15 TJS would carry up to 12 jammers in the FAST packs with no fuel, or six jammers in the packs with 4,450lb of fuel. The idea remains to remove the pallets and convert the aircraft back to an air superiority configuation.

With an 8,000 hours a year airframe life (which is climbing), MCAIR is only beginning to see the electronics additions for the F-15. It is considered by the company to be a capable aircraft for many of these missions. To give some idea of the additional missions being considered at MCAIR in addition to the ones already listed are the following: nuclear delivery with MK-57 nuclear tactical weapons, advanced strike with GBU-weapons, MK-84 laser guided bombs, advanced interceptor with AIM-54 Phoenix missiles and sea surveillance with Harpoon missiles.

7.
Modern Air Combat

The F-15 enters service to fight in an arena that has been the subject of controversy since the inception of the fighter aircraft. To attempt to understand the Eagle's mission without looking into modern air combat is difficult since the F-15's birth was predicated upon a fighter optimised for hard, close-in manoeuvring.

Hassling, dogfighting, mixing it up, was as much a part of aerial combat as the guns mounted in the aircraft up through World War 2 and Korea. In the late 1950s, however, the concept evolved, at least in the West, that missiles were replacing fixed cannon in air-to-air fighting. The next war would be one of ICBMs and long range bombers. The only projected need in fighter aircraft would, therefore, be a fast, high-flying interceptor armed with radar and long range missiles. The pilot would never see the aircraft he was shooting at. Thus were born the ideas that produced the F-4 Phantom II and F-106 Delta Dart.

As the F-4 and its Sparrow missile were introduced into the inventory, it was widely predicted they would eliminate air combat manoeuvring (ACM) because no fighter could escape a radar missile.

One of the first American offensives over North Vietnam, Rolling Thunder, was a painful slap in the face. From 1965 to 1968 110 MiG-17s and 21s were shot down in air-to-air engagements. The US lost 48 fighters for a resulting kill-to-loss ratio of 2.29:1. Compared to the Korean War's 7:1 or better, this was totally unacceptable. In the last months of Rolling Thunder up to November 1968, the Navy fired more than 50 missiles without one hit.

The close-in, visual, manoeuvring air battle had rudely come back on the scene. Since the F-4 was earmarked as a fleet defence fighter, the pilot was told not to pull more than 3g to avoid harming the delicate radar, so the F-8s engaged the MiGs. Since the F-8's guns would jam above 3g it was no real solution to the problem. In any case, the Navy had lost interest in single-seat fighters . . . the Crusader made its last kill in 1968 before being pulled out of combat. The Navy then launched the F-4s as air superiority fighters. By mid-1968 the Navy's Ault Report uncovered the fact that pilots were untrained for the classic manoeuvring fight, as well as suggesting there were problems elsewhere in missiles, radar, aircrews, planes. By September the Navy Fighter Weapons School was set up at NAS Miramar, California, nicknamed 'Top Gun'. A-4 Skyhawks simulated MiG-17s and F-8s MiG-21s. Air Force F-106s, also excellent Mig-21 simulators, were later flown in the programme through a 1970 Navy-Aerospace (then Air) Defense Command agreement.

The first 'Top Gun' graduates were into the sqaudrons by April 1969. The Navy's foresight paid off during April-December 1972 as Linebacker I and II reopened the aerial offensive over North Vietnam. The kill ratio went up to 12.5:1 for 1970-3, with most of the engagements taking place in 1972, according to the Navy.

The USAF's first dissimilar air combat tactics (DACT) programme was initiated by the Aerospace Defense Command in 1967. Up to this point most ACT training was, unrealistically enough, against an aircraft of the same type, the only variable being the pilot. The first instructors were trained at the USAF Fighter Weapons School at Nellis AFB, Nevada, as F-106s were flown against F-4s and F-100s. In 1968 the ADCOM ACT programme was transferred to the USAF Interceptor Weapons School at Tyndall AFB, Florida, called College Dart. The first joint service training exercise was conducted at Miramar between Air Force 84th Fighter Interceptor Squadron 106s and Navy VF-121 Phantoms. Today all three services 'fight' each other on a regular basis.

The Air Force found the air combat situation in Vietnam harder to solve. Following the USAF fighter-bomber or multi-mission tradition, TAC F-4s flew close air support, interdiction and air superiority. The Navy, having a tradition of separate fighter and attack specialties, freed F-4s for the air superiority mission while the A-4s, A-6s and A-7s did the bombing. At the end of Linebacker TAC's 1970-3 kill ratio was 2:1, even worse than the 1965-8 ratio.* The Air Force's own Red Baron Report on its MiG encounters came up with 'insufficient training and experience in air-to-air combat'.

Overall Air Force experience with the Sparrow was little different from the Navy; mostly less than 10%

*There were notable exceptions to this, such as the 432nd TRW at Udorn full of Fighter Weapons School graduates. Specialising in Combat Air Patrol, the Wing obtained 33 kills for five losses in 1972.

Above: A 32nd TFS Eagle out of Soesterburg, Netherlands on patrol near the West/East German border, loaded for bear. *MCAIR*

kills. Air Force Sidewinders, the AIM-9E and AIM-9J, on the other hand, got only about two-thirds the success rate of the Navy Sidewinders, the AIM-9B, D and G. 65% of the Sparrows and 45% of the Sidewinders malfunctioned due to launch, guidance or fusing failures.

Another interesting set of statistics arises from the breakdown of Air Force kills in South-East Asia. Throughout the war the USAF achieved 137 MiG kills against MiG-17s, 19s and 21s. The following weapons were responsible for these kills: Sparrow, 50; Sidewinder, 33; Sidewinder plus guns, 2; guns, 42; Falcon, 5; manoeuvring, 5. The majority of the kills can be attributed to the dogfight-type weapon. The number of kills made with Sidewinders and guns was 77. Add the manoeuvring kills to that, it comes to 82, add the infra-red homing Falcon and it comes to 87 of the 137 kills. Even more significant data results when one considers most of the Sparrow kills were made within visual range under manoeuvring conditions. The classic dogfight had returned . . . in actuality it had never left.

The 42 gun kills require a closer look. This is a much lower proportion of gun kills than the two-thirds the Israelis experienced in the 1973 War, due primarily to the F-4E being the only aircraft in the Vietnam War with an internal gun that would work at over 3g and with an air-to-air gunsight. It did not enter the war until 1968 and then only in wing strength.

Before Linebacker was over, TAC formed the 64th Fighter Weapons Sqaudron at Nellis in October 1972, with 18 T-38s, 22 aircrew and six weapons controllers. With the formation of this Air Force 'aggressor' squadron, the United States entered its first realistic training period for fighter pilots in 20 years.

With the advent of fighters that can fly at supersonic speeds there have been some modest changes in doctrine, tactics and formation, but it still holds true that the manoeuvring battle is still very much a part of fighter flying.

One of these changes has been the introduction of 'Loose Deuce' as the Navy calls it, tactical partnership or 'Fluid Two' to the Air Force. The 'welded wing' flying of wingman on leader is in disfavour. The rigid finger four doesn't find many adherents now, although the concept of fluid four and shooter-cover has not left. As a matter of fact, the latter has found a new resurgence of acceptance within the fighter community.

The combat spread formation widely used by 'Loose Deuce' practitioners as they enter a fight is flown in lateral separation of one nautical mile or more with 3-5,000ft vertical separation. An intrusion by an attacker requires only a break in one direction or the other to sandwich the opponent. No time is wasted in first splitting, then breaking. Each aircraft can easily clear the others 6 o'clock position, potentially being able to fight several adversaries as each clears the other. Both aircraft are effective fighters whereas the finger or fluid four can cut combat effectiveness by 50% in limiting the wingman. In this way of doing things, each aircraft can alternate between free fighter and engaged fighter. The free fighter repositions for another attack while taking the responsibility to clear his element for other bogies. This 'double attack' has its problems when excessive radio communications are required – chatter and jamming quickly take the radio away.

Left: A 36th Wing Eagle flies out on an ACT sortie with a 527th TFTAS F-5E aggressor. The Northrop Tiger II has done a fine job in simulating the MiG-21 during air combat training. *USAF*

Below: AIM-9 Sidewinders are brought up to the flight line at Bitburg. *USAF*

Bottom: Maj Tom Owens of the 1st TFW talks with S/Sgt David Peters and A1C Douglas McClay at Red Flag VIII in October 1976. Red Flag has proven to be one of the most successful realistic training scenarios ever developed, giving pilots valuable combat experience. *USAF*

Guns, superior manoeuvrability and excellent visibility are back in the fighters now. In Vietnam, until the F-4E came along, the guns had to be slung in pods under the aircraft to counter the MiGs. Pilots were also 'buried' in their aircraft with very poor rearward visibility.

Camouflage paint has also returned which takes into consideration the air-to-air arena. A 'lizard' ground scheme at altitude looks like a black silhouette. Current F-15s are painted in Compass Ghost Grey, making the aircraft more indistinct. Since it is a larger airplane, the use of paint, in many pilots' opinions, is very important. Aviation artist Keith Ferris has gone even further, having developed an innovative scheme of painting aircraft in deceptive ways so that they appear to be doing something they are not.

The aggressor squadrons in the Navy and Air Force have been the centre of the effort to get realistic training back into fighter flying. An example of aggressor squadron academics is a curriculum containing the following subjects: the Soviet fighter pilot, Soviet aircraft avionics and armament, Soviet air defence system, Soviet battle arena, Soviet fighter formations and tactics. The aggressors have trained radar controllers as well, thoroughly schooled in Soviet intercept tactics which call for close radar control of their fighters on all missions.

The Air Force aggressor pilots themselves have an average of 1,400 hours of fighter time with a wide variety of air-to-air experience. Continually required to fly as Soviet fighter pilots would, they give American pilots some very realistic training. Even the aircraft are painted in known communist bloc colour schemes, complete with red digit numbers on the fuselages.

The primary aggressor aircraft, the F-5E Tiger II in both the Navy and Air Force fighter weapons schools, possesses acceleration and turn rate, as well as

Right: A 36th Wing Eagle gets off on a Zulu scramble, fully armed, from Bitburg. The F-15s at Bitburg and Soesterburg are in front for interception of any incoming bogies. *USAF*

Below: A 32nd TFS F-15A has just responded to a scramble. Fully armed, this Eagle is one of two on constant alert at Soesterburg. *USAF*

weapons capability, similar to the MiG-21. The F-5E, for all intents and purposes, becomes the 21 in a fight, complete with gunsight and weapons.

The 57th Fighter Weapons Wing at Nellis has become the focal point of air combat training in the Air Force, complete with travelling 'road shows' that visit fighter, attack and reconnaissance bases. When the aggressors arrive at a base, participating air crews and weapons controllers receive a briefing on the entire programme. The aggressor squadron instructors then provide eight hours of academics.

Following right behind the formation of the aggressor squadrons was the creation of Red Flag, a major step forward in air tactics training. Throughout the time period of sophisticated weapons, from the F-100 on, the military has been careful about hurting their airplanes in peacetime. Aircraft are increasingly expensive now; when they are lost they cost a great deal of money to replace . . . pilots cost a great deal to train. So the emphasis up through the end of the Vietnam War became one of the safety at all costs, even at the cost of effective training.

To practice air combat manoeuvring, aircraft become exposed to a higher percentage of potentially dangerous situations. In a hard manoeuvring fight, the rules in today's arena call for a bubble of a thousand feet to be put around the aircraft that no one penetrates, but this often is not the case. There have been some collisions and losses. Vietnam revealed, however, that even more airplanes would be lost without effective training.

Tactical Air Commander Gen Robert J. Dixon was awarded the Collier Trophy for establishing Red Flag. In the exercise squadron-sized units deploy on a regular basis to Nellis for air combat training. Its purpose is to provide active duty, Air National Guard and Air Force Reserve aircrews with a realistic enemy threat in a training environment. Aircrews perform combat missions against an enemy force equipped with simulated surface-to-air missiles (SAMs) and

Above: An F-15 at Bitburg in its TABV hardened shelter. *USAF*

Left: On the range near Nellis for AOT training. *USAF*

anti-aircraft artillery (AAA). The opposition also commands two squadrons of aggressors.

The requirement of Red Flag training grew out of studies of aerial combat experience since World War 2 which reveal that a crewman's chances of survival increase dramatically after his first 10 combat missions. The Air Force is striving to give at least 10 'combat' missions to a pilot before he ever sees combat.

The electronic signals emitted from enemy SAM sites and AAA batteries are an important element in modern aerial battle, and aircrews must recognise them to take the proper evasive actions. The SAMs come complete with compressed air charges which 'poof' the desert, even though a missile does not leave the rail, for the pilot to see. If a pilot is 'shot down', often when he lands he is put in a helicopter, taken back out to the area where he was downed and then he jumps out with a parachute, or jumps out of the helicopter as it sets down. He then has to evade back to friendly territory. At the end of each day's simulated battles, through observer groups, scoring results are determined and critiques offered during thorough debriefings, probably the key factor in Red Flag's success since they are used to evaluate tactics employed during the day's missions and to correct any recognisable problems.

Above: In trail – this shot was taken from the Bicentennial F-15B Eagle, showing the excellent cockpit visibility. *MCAIR*

Aircrews have a chance to hear 'the enemy's' assessment of their skill when the members of the aggressor squadron and ground threat operators present their evaluations.

Red Flag has been so successful that it has expanded in scope to include aircrews from Strategic Air Command, Military Airlift Command, all phases of Tactical Air Command, as well as units from the Army, Navy and Marine Corps. In addition, representatives from Great Britain, West Germany, Canada, Australia, Korea and New Zealand have flown at Red Flag.

Since Red Flag began in November 1975 it has grown to the point where the sortie total of some exercises has reached 2,400 with as many as 250 sorties a day. TAC tries to get its units there at least once every 12 months, to stay for two or more weeks. Admittedly, the Red Flag exercise is a clear weather scenario and central European weather is not nearly as agreeable. However, the Air Force is making an effort to duplicate Warsaw Pact air and ground defensive threat systems that create a realistic battle field environment. Pilots, within certain limits, are urged to try new tactics they think will improve their chances of evading the threats that are deployed against them. As many limits as possible are taken off so that they can actually experience what it means to be in combat.

The ranges at Nellis extend about 140 miles north of the base and are about 170 miles wide, which include an air combat manoeuvring instrumentation range of 30 miles diameter air space, monitored by an advanced electronic tracking system. A total of 27 threat simulators ranging from replicas of Soviet early warning radars to tracking and acquisition radars of SAMs and anti-aircraft guns are deployed in the two threat areas. There are several live ordnance ranges, including an airfield constructed like a base in East Germany with F-86s to simulate MiGs.

To say all this is realistic would be an understatement. A pilot experiencing combat soon forgets that the aircraft pursuing him is flown by the friendly pilot in the bar last night. Instead it becomes an actual MiG and the pilot has to do everything he can to survive first of all, and then possibly to shoot his 'enemy' down. (The F-5s are very hard to see with an average 1.6-mile visual acquisition. What this amounts to is surprise, particularly when the F-15 and the F-14 can be seen from about 10 miles out or more.)

To give some idea of what goes on at a Red Flag as far as the scope of the operation, Red Flag 79-9 was held in August and September 1979. 12 F-15s from the 49th Tac Fighter Wing at Holloman were the main players with an air-to-air role in the first Red Flag to run a total of six weeks. The F-16 and F-14 were deployed, as well as the Republic of Korea flying F-5Es. The following chart gives the scope of this programme:

Red Flag 79-9

	Aircraft	*Unit*	*Base*
USAF	12 F-15 Eagles	49th TFW	Holloman AFB, NM (primary unit)
	F-4Gs & F-105s	35th TFW	George AFB, CA
	6 A-10 Thunderbolts	354th TFW	Myrtle Beach AFB, SC
	3 0-2s	27th TASS	Davis-Monthan AFB, AZ
	F-5E aggressors	57th TFTW	Nellis AFB, NV
	1 E-3A Sentry	522nd AWCW	Tinker AFB, OK
	F-111Ds	27th TFW	Cannon AFB, NM
	F-111As	366th TFW	Mountain Home AFB, ID
ANG	8 A-7 Corsairs	114th TFG	South Dakota
	4 A-7 Corsairs	162nd TFTG	Arizona
	6 F-4 Phantoms	915th TFG	Florida
	12 A-7 Corsairs	138th TFG	Oklahoma
	4 RF-4 Phantoms	187th TRG	Alabama
	4 RF-4 Phantoms	123rd TRW	Kentucky
USAF	F-16s	57th TTW	Hill AFB, UT
	EF-111s	AFTAWC	Mountain Home AFB, ID
	F-106s	84th FIS	Castle AFB, CA
	8 C-130s	MAC	
	4 C-141s	MAC	
	2 UH-1s	MAC	
	B-52Gs	SAC	
	KC-135s	SAC	
	FB-111s	SAC	
USN	F-4Js		
	F-14s		
	A-4s		
	A-6s		
	A-7s		
	AH-1Ts		
USMC	F-4Ns		
Korea	F-5Es		

Thrown in to this enormous battle, the F-15 and its pilots are gaining a great deal of experience, which has been the idea ever since Red Flag started. The F-15 and Red Flag seem to have grown up together and pilots have become very aware of their strong points and weaknesses.

Maj D. L. Smith of the 64th Aggressor Squadron led the first aggressor deployment to Luke for operations with the F-15 Operational Test and Evalution Unit (OT&E). His recollections of that first encounter with the Eagle are worth quoting:

'Since the F-15 owns the turn advantage in almost all cases, turn early against an opponent that has allowed any lateral spacing. When an adversary overshoots, reverse early. Discard the sequential attack concept since the F-15 can outperform any known Soviet aircraft one versus one. Do not follow the F-4 initial move concept of the man under attack extends while the free fighter pitches into the bandit. Rather, the F-15 under attack will hard turn to force the overshoot while the free F-15 moderate turns to save energy in the event the bandit attempts to separate . . . In one vs one engagements I have never fought so long and so hard with no thought of gaining an advantage, but rather to keep from being shot. From a head on pass followed by three hard turns, the F-15 will be approaching some type of weapons parameters. Once the F-15 is behind the three-nine line (3 o'clock, 9 o'clock positions on the attacked aircraft) and pointing at you, your problems are severe since you can neither outrun him or outturn him. The Soviets employ a violent manoeuvre called the Jink-Out as a defence against an opponent in a gun position. Heading toward the sun is also an excellent defensive move. I have never jinked-out nor headed toward the sun so many times in my life.

'No aircraft is perfect, however, and certainly no pilot is perfect, so there were shots called against the F-15, but that is why the aggressor mission has been of such worth. For example: most shots were in the two vs one environment where it is extremely difficult for a single aircraft to engage two well coordinated opponents successfully.

'One F-15 pilot felt that a near vertical climb would be an effective move against an attacker at 6 o'clock. With a short lag followed by a hard pull, the T-38 had excellent "Atoll" parameters (the "Atoll" is the Soviet Sidewinder). After evaluation, a 15° to 30° climb with a slight turn will drop an attacker back to a distance where the F-15 can hard turn for a head-on pass. Even with the occasional mistakes made, the F-15 proved almost impossible to fight one on one. The performance characteristics are so good that new tactical concepts will certainly come to light.'

The F-15's performance has dictated a change in tactics. The Eagle can easily sustain a 5g turn without losing any airspeed. It can work the vertical like no other aircraft except the F-16 while maintaining speed, preferably over 350kts. This is due, in essence, to the high thrust-to-weight ratio.

The F-15 pilot has an instantaneous turn rate of more than 16°/sec in changing direction and a sustained turn in the F-15 can be done at more than 14°/sec. This compares to about 11°/sec sustained for the F-5E. The Eagle can sustain 7.3g in afterburner at 400kts at 15,000ft with no loss of airspeed. There are basically no trim changes throughout the envelope of the aircraft as well. It is an easy aircraft to fly according to the pilots, but it does take much ground school and practice to operate the weapons control system.

Essentially very little has changed concerning the fundamental dynamics of air-to-air fighting since World War 2, or even World War 1 for that matter. Increasing complexity of both airframes, avionics and power plants does not antiquate the hard close-in manoeuvring fight. As John Boyd has so often stated, aerial combat is fundamentally an open-ended, manoeuvre/counter-manoeuvre process, fluid in the extreme.

Many fighter thinkers have laid their careers on the line at various points to ram home this fact, a fact that as of yet has not been disproven by actual combat, yet is continually being hammered away at by people who would wish to disprove it with theories and potential scenarios.

Along with John Boyd, Everest Riccioni, author of *Tigers Airborne* which originated the double attack system, and Pierre Sprey continue to call for what is effective in the air-to-air arena regardless of its complexity, its cost, or anything else. What they have asked for are continuing studies on an aircraft that doesn't cost a great deal, is not very complex, flies

Below: October 1979 – The 33rd had a chance to exercise its Eagles at Maple Flag in Canada. This bird is returning to the line, full of F-104s, after a mission. *USAF*

Right: Maple Flag, like the USAF's Red Flag, gave the 33rd Wing a chance to deploy to Canada from Florida for some realistic training. *USAF*

Left: The 'Compass Ghost' grey camouflage scheme was standardised after Air Superiority Blue was dropped. Air-to-air paint is still a topic of much discussion and there will no doubt be more schemes applied as time goes on. *MCAIR*

Right: October 1979 – a 33rd TFW F-15A taxies out at Eglin AFB, Florida for an ACT sortie. Note the aggressor F-5s in the background. *MCAIR*

often, is hard to see . . . and that can be bought in large numbers.

According to Sprey, combat derived effectiveness criteria arrange themselves in the following order of priority: (1) achieve surprise bounces without being surprised (from World War 1 to Vietnam 65-86% of all air-to-air losses were shot down unaware); (2) outnumber the enemy in the air (70 vastly superior Me262s were 'ground down' by 2,000 inferior P-47s and P-51s); (3) outmanoeuvre the enemy to gain firing position always dominated by pilot ability/training; energy manoeuvrability plus transient performance; (4) achieve reliable kills during any split second opportunity (air combat has always required visual identification; the more aircraft engaged, the more fleeting the firing opportunities).

One of the major problems facing current thinking is the lack of lethality in air-to-air weapons. Now that guns are finally back in the aircraft there has been frustration over the 20mm, the standard gun in all today's modern fighters, not being as effective as the old .50 calibre that it replaced. This is due to the 20mm's poor ballistics, small explosive load and inacceptably poor fusing. The .50 calibre also had a greater rate of fire initially than the 20mm. The reason for this is the difference in drive – the gatling cannon has a motor that must come up to speed to fire at full rate (6,000 rounds per minute) while the .50 calibre machine gun was gas driven so it had an instantaneous rate of fire. It is interesting to note that in the first second the eight guns of a P-47 fired, they put out roughly 120 rounds compared to about 75 from the F-15's 20mm Vulcan. The cannon, however, is less prone to jamming.

In assessing combat kills per trigger squeeze (P_k or probability of kill), the figures note that gun lethality has gone consistently down since World War 2, so that during the Vietnam War the P_k was 0.26 kills per trigger squeeze with the M61 20mm cannon (in 1972 and 1973 the F-4E got 0.5, however). In Korea the P_k with .50 calibres in F-86s and other aircraft was 0.31 when the computing gun sight was working and 0.34 when it wasn't working. In World War 2, kill ratios against fighters were even higher at about 0.4 or 0.5. This is more interesting when one notes that 80% of those aircraft downed by rounds of 40mm or less calibre were due to fire or hydraulic failure, not to mechanical damage, which again says something about the importance of incendiary qualities rather than explosive effect.

In Vietnam the AIM-7 Sparrow, in spite of three major model changes from the D to the E to the E2, was never improved in P_k: all models got between 0.08 to 0.1.* The AIM-9, the Sidewinder, got about twice the lethality of the Sparrow – still not very high but at least respectable, considering the low cost of the missile and the much lower weight/complexity penalty it imposes on the fighter. The first model, the AIM-9B, got a P_k of 0.15; the improved AIM-9D came along and showed some improvement with a 0.19 P_k.

The point is to compare this kill lethality with that of the aircraft gun. Improvement has not been

*The kill ratios for the AIM-7 in Vietnam were arrived at by tabulating 55 kills out of 589 firing attempts. It was 31 kills out of 325 attempts when the target was straight ahead and only 30° off either side of the nose, which are ideal parameters.

realised and missiles, if anything, have brought lethality down. The significance of this lies in the continual insistance that the missile is the most effective weapon mounted on aircraft, particularly in beyond visual range engagements. In Vietnam the US tried beyond visual range engagements and shot down several of its own fighters by failing to identify the target visually. There has been a great deal of work on improving the IFF (the transponder that identifies a friendly fighter) in airplanes, but transponders and avionics are neither foolproof nor secure from enemy spoofing. It still comes down to putting an eye on the target before firing, as in previous wars.

Missiles have extended killing ranges, but not beyond visual range in most cases, complementing rather than replacing guns. If anything missiles have increased the need to turn once fired upon. In World War 2 even a slight top speed advantage would enable the pilot to disengage from the fight, but the non-manoeuvring disengagement is impossible when a missile is coming down on one's tail. The pilot's only option is to pull very hard to get it to miss. This puts him back into a hard manoeuvring fight and if anything the gun at that point becomes the primary weapon. For the future some thinkers are proposing a high velocity, high incendiary .50 calibre as a superior weapon to the 20mm.

Above: A 33rd Wing F-15 – note distinctive eagle's head crest. *MCAIR*

There is an underlying conflict that very few people see between what the technology advocates and industry want to build – to spend money on, to get appropriations for – and what the actual operational needs of the fighter fleet are.

The AIMVAL/ACEVAL tests of January to October 1977 are the most recent attempts by the military services to gain an understanding of air-to-air combat. AIMVAL was to examine five missile concepts, whereas ACEVAL was set up to examine force size ratios and how they would affect the outcome of a dogfight.

Blue Forces fought Red Forces, the former composed of F-14s and F-15s, the latter composed of F-5Es simulating MiG-21s. For the ACEVAL portion of the test, the Blue Force was configured with AIM-7F Sparrows and AIM-9L Sidewinders along with 20mm guns while the Red Force had short range Sidewinders and 20mm guns.

The evaluators slowly graduated the force size from one vs one to four vs four, with the rules of engagement calling for visual identification. Again, there was some controversy about the fact that this did not include the beyond visual range type of fight, therefore not allowing the F-14 or F-15 to utilise radar guided missiles.

Out of the ACEVAL tests perhaps the most significant finding was that as the total number of airplanes increased in the battle, the exchange ratio in favour of the F-14/F-15 declined. One F-15 versus the F-5 resulted in an exchange ratio of slightly greater than 3:1 in favour of the F-15.* When four F-15s engaged four F-5Es the kill-loss ratio went down to about 1.5:1.

One of the Navy pilots involved in the tests made the following statement, 'I do not feel that the way we are presently configured hardware-wise and training-wise, we could reasonably expect to have the exchange ratios that we enjoyed in Vietnam (1970-2) and Korea. By that I mean approaching 10:1.'

When the F-15s were outnumbered 2:1 then the exchange ratio drastically decreased down to close to 1:1. The man in the cockpit cannot be overtaxed to do his job, and the more complex the equipment, the more one has to monitor a number of different things, the harder it is going to be to survive.

'During a VF-121 debriefing at "Top Gun", the following was noted: "A most usual result of cockpit 'magic' is to have a sophisticated aircraft (in a multi-bogey environment) plunge through a gaggle concentrating on his target, going for a (slow) Sparrow kill, oblivious to the rest of the aircraft and getting recorded as – 'killed while killing'." '

After the AIMVAL/ACEVAL test crews came out with some very different interpretations of what resulted than those made by some of the observers. They made it a point to exploit weapon system weaknesses as well as any split second tactical weaknesses or mistakes displayed by their adversaries. This came down to remaining unpredictable. GCI controllers were able to help single aircraft to win, but as the engagements changed from one vs one to four vs four, the radar controllers found out they couldn't cope regardless of the capability of their radar systems. In such situations the engagements tended to degenerate into every-man-for-himself in a many-versus-many environment. Communications became saturated, the two man crew concept seemed to fall apart and the value of a sophisticated weapons system went unused. This was a major finding and one that was not particularly surprising to many people who knew what would happen. Tactics, numbers and being hard to see created the winners. The need arose for systems that provide the ability to detect, identify, point, shoot and extend more quickly than an adversary. Training became an important point. Most agreed that the complex weapon systems provided more tactical options but took longer for the aircrew to learn how to operate it properly and exploit its potential. They found that even untrained men, at least untrained in the F-5, were able to go out with the aggressors and within weeks win consistently, which emphasised that training to a high proficiency level could be accomplished quickly given relatively simple systems.

The aggressor pilots began consistently to determine the range from an F-15 or F-14 at which their aircraft became 'invisible', while at the same time the F-15 or F-14 was visible. Aggressor pilots became aware of what the F-15 radar could do to them, especially in look-down, shoot-down capability. They devised many innovative tactics to defeat the radars, including lock-breaking manoeuvres, crossing tracks and zero doppler turns. This came out of some 2,300 sorties pitting F-15s and F-14s against F-5s which were flown in both the missile concept and tactics phases.

Maj Barry D. Watts did a great deal of research into just this problem in 1979 at the Pentagon. In his paper, 'Fire, Movement and Tactics', he brought out the following conclusion: 'The most powerful source of friction in aerial combat seems to lie in the complexity which sharply separates true multiple participant encounters such as six versus six, from isolated one versus one, and two versus one scenarios.'

*This ratio was normalised over GCI states. In some one vs one fights, the F-15s scored as high as 18:1.

It seemed the aircrews were able to keep track of all the other airplanes in the fight in the one versus one and one versus two fights, but with 10 or 12 aircraft in one piece of sky constant awareness of all the participants became impossible. Or was Watts put it, 'The problem of staying alive becomes harder and harder as the number of planes involved goes up.'

In one versus one, the Eagle's advantages in weaponry and manoeuvrability were so overwhelming, as the aggressors had found earlier, that the aircraft would win most of the time. Experience began to show that as the number of participants increased, the raw hardware advantages which make the F-15 so overwhelming against earlier generation aircraft became less and less important.

By mid-1978 aggressors and Eagles were going up in great numbers. Sometimes six versus six or four F-5s versus six F-15s and this found the Eagles unable to sustain a 2:1 kill ratio advantage.

Lee Harrell, who participated as an aggressor pilot, made these comments: 'Once we got into the "knife fighting" portion the F-15's kill ratio was distinctly less than 1:1. Overall, with no visual identification required prior to shooting, it was slightly better than 1:1, but once the fight matured, the Eagle died like everyone else.'

With 10 to 12 planes in the arena Harrell found himself only rarely able to cycle through the basic manoeuvre patterns which usually decided one versus one contests. Instead the crowded environment forced a look-shoot-break-look style of fighting. Watts went on to say, 'So rapidly did the threat arrays each pilot was trying to cope with change, that the pattern of individual manoeuvre became fragmented and jerky. Sustained manoeuvring against a given adversary for any length of time – even for just 20 or 30 seconds – only served by and large to give some other opponent a shot. Thus the tempo and rhythm of multi-participant engagements are fundamentally different from those representative of isolated aircraft limited encounters. To survive in the face of substantial numbers of participants, aircrews have to employ more irregular, faster-developing, less predictable patterns of manoeuvre.'

Pilots were finding as well that 'Loose Deuce', which had become very much the true faith for the jet age believers trained in one vs one and two vs two, was now giving way to the shooter-cover approach. Not the welded wing of the past, but a cover man who could help prevent surprise while watching in the middle of a gaggle of enemy fighters.

Watts again pointed out, 'As AIMVAL/ACEVAL documented at length, the key to survival in air-to-air lies in being able to recognise when and where a specific tactic will succeed, not in simply pulling the same trick out of a tactical bag each and every time you run into a given kind of situation. And few fighter pilots ever believed that "Loose Deuce" would give way back to the shooter-cover concept, but it has proven to be happening over the deserts of Nevada,' the point being not to go back to shooter-cover so much as to insist it shouldn't be thrown away.

The concept that John Boyd synthesised from 25 years of jet combat training and testing is that victory is created by being able to 'observe-orient-decide-act' faster than the enemy. Regardless of what manoeuvre or counter-manoeuvre is required, or what system is working or isn't working, that is what must be done.

The idea, then, according to Boyd is that going through the observe-orient-decide-act loop faster than the enemy produces disorientation and then panic in the opponent. This is done by being quick, ambiguous and deceptive in one's actions, giving the opponent an impression of events as they are not. Boyd makes this point in his 'Patterns of Conflict' briefing, an overview of military history that reveals these ideas were inherent in the victories of great commanders back to Alexander. The same ideas underlie Sprey's four combat derived effectiveness criteria.

In the January 1979 issue of *Air Force* Magazine General T. R. Milton, USAF (Ret), wrote an article entitled 'Reflections from Red Flag'. His points are fascinating considering they were made from his on-the-spot observations as an experienced Air Force pilot:

'Maybe we have made too much of the machinery in our natural desire to have the best airplane. As Red Flag proves day after day, an expert in an F-5 can give anyone, no matter what he is flying, a very hard time. Expertly flown, an F-4 is still a great airplane and more than a match for anything less expertly flown. Then there is the matter of numbers. The best fighter pilot in the world – there are of course countless claimants to that title – flying the best airplane, is still going down if he is sufficiently outnumbered by almost any sort of fighter armed with a reliable missile. Numbers are something we are short of in this era where the cost per pound of a modern fighter is becoming competitive with that of precious metals . . . Since the Red Flag exercises have made a case for the importance of numbers, something which we have always known but tend to forget, it may be worthwhile to think a bit about the possibilities of some low cost, low sophistication – well, relatively any way – augmentations to the high cost fighters. An F-15 to do the target spotting, some little friends to help out with the fight . . . Enough Me109s could still win the day over not enough F-4s just as an

overwhelming force of P-51s negated the one-sided performance superiority of the Luftwaffe's jets during the end of World War 2. The need for numbers of aircraft and reliable and flexible armament seems to be Red Flag's conclusion. Unhappily armament development has clearly lagged behind airplane development, with a resulting failure to realise everything the airplane/pilot combination is capable of. There is need for an all-aspect missile . . . called the Bruno. One simply has to squeeze the trigger and give the command, "Go, Bruno! Kill!"'

Milton was disturbed with his realisation that our forces are very thin and that we probably don't have sufficient spare parts to sustain any high intensity operation. He realised that the US needed operations and maintenance money, war reserve munitions, and sufficient aircraft and pilot replacements which complexity has a tendency to reduce. The extreme cost of our weapon systems has driven the force size down from the sorties per day per million dollars that were generated in the 1950s. Excessive avionics requirements are doubling the size of today's fighter and multiplying its cost. This is disturbing considering many are saying that these avionics have much poorer lethality than the old weapons of the past.

In essence, it is being said the US is in a Catch-22 situation . . . the more complex, the more capable the system, the less we can buy and the less lethal it is due to inherent problems. There was once a time, from 1955 to 1965 when technology enthusiasts believed so strongly in the invincibility of air-to-air missiles that they favoured subsonic transport-type, long range missile launching aircraft as fighters (this has also been proposed recently). Today's Phoenix missile system is the direct product of this concept, coming out of the Navy's cancelled Missileer 'fighters' and Eagle missile.

In 1968 Pierre Sprey made a number of significant conclusions that continue to stand the test of time in his staff study entitled *The Impact of Avionics on the Effectiveness of Tactical Air:*

'Current and past avionics effectiveness analyses and predictions have failed to show any correlation with combat results; both claimed accuracies and P_k have been off (always in the same direction) by as much as an order of magnitude. Until the methodologies and data inputs used for such analyses demonstrate at least rough correlation with combat results, they will continue to be scientifically invalid and useless for decision making purposes.

'Peacetime testing procedures and organisational motivations that allow systems as ineffective and unreliable as some of those we now have in combat to proceed into inventory can and should be reformed. Test environments should not be created to show equipments to their best advantage; these environments should simply use tactical experience to reproduce the most stringent aspects of the combat situation.'

To say that this has been difficult to face in the defence community would be an understatement. When the Belenko MiG-25 defected to Japan, there was a great deal of publicity about how crude the aircraft was, with such things as vacuum tube avionics, heavy steel construction, and other unsophisticated items. It was a typical western reaction, but those in the Defense Department who have spent a great deal of time analysing Soviet air power stood in resect of the MiG-25 which can be

57th TTW F-15s at Nellis AFB, NV. The 57th serves as the USAF's Fighter Weapons School with a history that goes back to the F-86. The yellow and black checkerboard flash on the tail has been on the aircraft of this elite unit since the 1950s. *USAF*

built at far less cost than our comparable high performance aircraft.

The United States pays several times the amount the Soviets pay in building such airplanes. The Soviets have been able to keep costs down and therefore build greater numbers of fighters and bombers, whereas the West, with its greater technology and complexity, has been forced to build fewer aircraft with greater capability.*

Complex and costly weapons have an adverse effect on training, both for pilots and for ground crews. In testimony before the committee on Armed Services in Congress Charles E. Myers, Jr, former Assistant Deputy Director, Defense Research and Engineering, made the following statements in regard to the fiscal year 1979 and 1980 defence budgets:

'In view of the demonstration of ills of the multi-purpose all-weather syndrome, it seems incredible that responsible military and civilian factions can continue to call for increased sophistication in all fighters. Instead they should be encouraging the design of less sophisticated versions with the hope of lowering cost and reversing the downward trends in equipment, crew readiness and force size. The really discouraging aspect of it all is that Congress, while emphasising the necessity to improve military strength and in the face of popular demand for decreased spending, continues to be victimised by a technology cartel which conjure new promises and portray deterrence as a contest in technological

*This issue is far from clear, however, since solid data is virtually nonexistent. Soviet aircraft could very well cost less because more are built. There is also controversy over the 2:1 numbers superiority of the Warsaw Pact, many saying that when counted in a different manner, the ratio comes down to 1:1.

sophistication unrelated to combat utility, force size and readiness . . . We are trying to rely on technological sophistication to bail us out of a problem. This has failed. As I said in the beginning during my tenure, I guess I failed along with everybody else. I finally yielded to the argument that said this time it is going to be better. Technology is really going to solve it for us this time.'

In referring to procurement costs of aircraft, Myers went on to analyse the cost trends in procuring tactical aircraft with the following constants: all fiscal year 1980 dollars with procurement of 500 aircraft for each type so as to stabilise the comparison. The trend in constant 1981 dollars is a continuous climb from under $250,000 for such aircraft as the P-51 through $5million for the F-104, to upwards of over $25million for the F-14 and the proposed all-weather interdiction Enhanced Tactical Fighter. The F-15 comes somewhere just over $15million while the A-10, the F-16 and the A-7 come between $5 and $10million. There is also a question mark at the bottom of the chart for the proposed 'blitzfighter', an austere, simple, jet powered aircraft that could serve as a tank killer and close air support machine.

'You can see where that is taking us. I have added to this chart two question marks such as what is our future direction. Are we going to continue to an even more sophisticated area? Do we go to a $35million Enhanced Tactical Fighter to do the night all-weather strikes, or battlefield interdiction, or should we try to go to a less than $5million plane? This is the problem Congress faces and the dilemma. If we are going to coninue in this direction, we will not have enough planes; we will end up with a token air force.'

One of the points Myers made was that the average fighter pilot is now training between 15 and 17 hours a month, whereas he really needs a great deal more than this to remain current in his machine. 'One of the things we do is end up buying fewer planes because they are more expensive. Our pilots don't train enough time in them. I think it has been demostrated at one of our Red Flag exercises that, yes, even an F-15 can be overwhelmed at some point with superior numbers and superior training.'

The matter in air combat is not how much the weapon is possibly capable of doing, but what it will actually do in combat. The scenarios that are predominant will determine what will kill what. 'In other words, can one shoot BVR most of the time while avoiding the manoeuvring arena?' says Barry Watts. 'If not, then a mainly F-15 fleet is not desirable: maybe a few F-15s and many F-5/YF-16 (F-16 prototype) type machines will work out much better.' It is not a matter of defence spending since currently the trend in the West is to reconsider the Soviet threat and to spend money to meet that threat. The point is how the money is spent and whether the force it is spent on is effective. Pierre Sprey's combat effectiveness trend summary in his 'Century Series' fighter briefing makes the following points:

'Since the F-86 our aircraft (except F-5 and F-16) have significantly decreased in abilty to achieve surprise bounces due to increases in size, smoke and emissions. Unnecessary increases in complexity and cost have decreased the effective force size per constant dollars by factors of 25 to 100 since the F-86. In dogfight performance one 'g' P_s (available excess power) has not improved significantly since the F-104A. Large deterioration in max 'g' is somewhat reversed by F-15 and F-16. Standard measures (or flight tests) of transient performance at high 'g' do not exist. Only F-86, F-5 and F-16 have attained excellent transient performance (this refers to how quickly a fighter can change from one manoeuvre to the next and therefore gain the advantage before the other fighter knows what is happening).

'Gun lethality (and range) has deteriorated since World War 2/Korea calibre .50 machine guns. Infra-red missile lethality in combat was one half of gun lethality; radar missile lethality was one-half that of infra-red missiles – despite continuous missile research and development since 1948.

'Current AIM-7 and AIM-9 modifications show no sign of fundamentally increasing missile lethality.'

In talking to these fighter analyists, what seems to be so frustrating for them is trying to propose what in their minds is the most effective force for the nation's defences. The more line pilots interviewed, the more their exerience seems to support Sprey's conclusions. What happens in combat does not seem to be consistant with the development and research interests of the defence R&D officials or the aerospace companies.

In 1979 there was a great deal of talk about the US re-examining its fighter needs. When confronting the numerically superior enemy forces that can be mustered by the Warsaw Pact, it seems the major emphasis was on alleged Soviet development of new 'stand-off' air superiority fighters and a new penetrating bomber. Questions were being raised as to the feasibility of the lightweight, clear air fighter of the F-16 class. This is why the F-14 found such impassioned advocates in the defence community as the new Air Force interceptor due to its superior long range weapons system. There were also recommendations to increase the complexity of the F-16 to a beyond visual range capability and two-seat F-15s with the Tomcat's Hughes Phoenix air-to-air missile system. Heavy emphasis was placed on the Enhanced Tactical Fighter, later called the Strike Eagle, or F-15E as a night, adverse weather, deep interdiction aircraft which would basically serve in the air-to-ground role.

Clarence A. Robinson, Jr, in an article in the 23 April 1979 issue of *Aviation Week,* went so far as to make the following statement, 'Data from the year-long air combat and missile evaluation tests over the Nevada desert between F-14s, F-15s and Northrop F-5 aggressor aircraft (AIMVAL/ACEVAL) tended to show that in most engagements when both enemy and friendly pilots engaged one another in dogfights within the lethal missile envelopes of both pilots, both are destroyed. Thus close-in dogfights may be a thing of the past, according to Pentagon officials.' In light of the lessons learned from Vietnam (and wars back to World War 1 for that matter), this has been a shock to the fighter pilots who are in the cockpit. Once again, military leadership is saying dogfighting is an obsolete mission. One analysis of ACEVAL showed that manoeuvring arena 1) expanded with all-aspect missiles and 2) became harder to avoid. It is the old Siren Song to give up manoeuvring in favour of technology.

The threat of the Backfire bomber with a range that can be extended over 7,000 nautical miles with a single in-flight refuelling has also figured into the picture since this puts beyond visual range combat back into the thinking of defence planners' minds. Ironically, this is the very same thinking that developed the F-4. It is not that the capabilities shouldn't be existent to fight in this manner. However, as complexity takes another leap, planners seem to be deserting the close-in hard manoeuvring fight for the beyond visual range fight. One of the motivations for saying that combat will be primarily a beyond visual range type of scenario is the bad weather in Europe, but there was no shortage of bad weather in Vietnam. Yet that war saw essentially nothing but visual bombing and visual air combat.

The Israelis have been the primary source for current air-to-air encounters since the 1973 Yom Kippur War dealt primarily with air superiority. The Israeli Air Force was unable to eliminate Arab air power as it had in 1967 due to the bomb-proof aircraft shelters and a traditionally effective use of AAA and SAMS. The systems were all Soviet built. The Israelis were forced to achieve aerial superiority through air-to-air combat as a result, but less than seven (none according to Gen Mordechai Hod, IAF Commander) of the 335 kills achieved by the Israelis in 1973 were made with Sparrows from beyond visual range. About two-thirds of the kills were with cannon; the remainder were obtained by Sidewinder or Shafrir missiles during air combat.

Respect for the Israeli Air Force among fighter pilots is high. The following statements from one of their air combat manoeuvring handbooks illustrates some of the IAF philosophy in flying fighters successfully:

'Our strength is based mainly on the pilot and not on the weapon system . . . Top grade pilots will achieve magnificent results even with less superior aircraft, but the bad pilot in a good aircraft has no impact upon the aircraft's characteristics. Moreso, there is a great probability that the pilot will kill himself . . .

'Don't let go of the (gun) trigger with first hits, but hold on till blowing up . . .

'The main problem in ACM of most aircraft is *where to* fly. To which place in the sky should the aircraft be flown in order to gain a relatively better

Left: An Israel Air Force F-15B, belonging to the 133rd Fighter Squadron, comes up fully armed to escort an F-15A in US markings in to Israel, completing a delivery. So far Israel has purchased 40 Eagles for $907 million (FY 80 dollars).

position over the rival aircraft, and to improve the position to kill position. The problem of *how to* fly the aircraft is of secondary importance . . .

'In training ACM, gun kills have much higher priority than missile kills (because, among other reasons) missile probability of kill is less than probability of kill by guns.'

Israeli F-15s bore out these conclusions in 1979 as Israel began to make pre-emptive strikes into Lebanon against terrorist strongholds. The scene was being set for the F-15's first experience in combat.

On several occasions the Syrians had come fairly close to Israeli aircraft, but never within missile range nor in an aggressive stance. On 27 June 1979 8-12 Syrian MiG-21bis fighters were ambushed by a force of six Israeli F-15s and two Kfirs. The Israeli Eagles had been scrambled over Haifa to cover a decoy flight of fighter bombers near Damour, Sidon and Tyre in southern Lebanon while guided by E-2C early warning aircraft. At 11 am, within three minutes six Syrian MiGs were shot down during a dogfight and several others were damaged. All of the kills were within visual range, four of them attributed to heat seeking missiles, one to a Sparrow and another to a gun; a Kfir was credited with one of the heat seeking missile kills according to an Israeli Air Force spokesman who was close to the event.

Ironically the second wave of F-15s almost got shot from behind because they were relying on the E-2C to get them warnings on stray Syrian MiGs. The Israeli pilots avoided this rearward threat through proper look-out doctrine which was ingrained by constant practice.

On 19 September 1979 the Syrians were again seeking combat when a MiG-23, or a MiG-25, according to other sources, used for the first time in combat, fired air-to-air missiles in attempting to down an Israeli RF-4 Phantom II without success. Five days later on the 24th Israeli intelligence revealed that the Syrians were again going to attempt an intercept against reconnaissance aircraft. Eagles, flying high altitude Combat Air Patrol, were vectored by a

Below: Israel's first Eagle arrives much to the delight of IAF pilots and families. Israel bought the first four Eagles out of pre-production Category II airframes [they were numbers F-14, F-15, F-16 and F-18]. *MCAIR*

Grumman E-2C to bounce four MiG-21s. In a close-in manoevring battle, all four MiGs were shot down.

There has been controversy as to whether any of the kills were made beyond visual range, but, in fact, the same old rules of visual identification applied as the Israelis ended up within visual range to get their 10 kills.

Conflict in Europe is possibly the best illustration of a future fight that might involve larger numbers of aircraft. In 1978 Lt-Gen H. J. Fish, Assistant Vice Chief of Staff, USAF, made the following statement: 'The rapid and continuing introduction of third generation offensive aircraft – such as the MiG-23/27, the MiG-21 J/K/L, and the Su-24 – provides the Pact with the capability to deliver air munitions deep within NATO Europe including the United Kingdom.* Likewise the Soviets are making major modernisation improvements in all the other required elements of tactical air warfare support. These elements include a well defended infrastructure with adequate bases for a larger wartime force and a capable, redundant and survivable command and control network. Similarly their impressive electronic warfare forces and equipment – both offensive and defensive – and their chemical war fighting capability will present serious challenges to NATO's current conventional defence capabilities. There have been two noticeable trends in Warsaw Pact air forces since 1974. First, while the numbers of combat aircraft have remained much the same over the last four years, there has been a marked increase in the numbers of aircraft capable of both defensive and offensive operations, or multi-role aircraft. Representing a substantially improved tactical offensive capability, the quality of the new offensive aircraft enables targets to be attacked at a much greater range than before and with roughly twice the weapons load of previous aircraft.

*Once again, it should be noted that there remain differing points of view on what constitutes a realistic Soviet threat. The above aircraft in reality do not have much range, particularly the MiG-21, and the 'Fencer' is not that long legged either. Frontal Aviation does not practise going deep – that mission belongs to Long Range Aviation.

Below: A 133rd IAF Fighter Squadron Eagle just airborne clean with the exception of a centreline tank. *MCAIR*

Above: Fully armed, on patrol, an Israel Air Force F-15 of the 133rd Fighter Squadron. *MCAIR*

'The second trend is the large increase in the number of armed assault helicopters. Soviet doctrine places considerable emphasis on the use of helicopters for landing assault troops and for providing them with fire support. Some of the latest Soviet helicopters are the most heavily armed in the world and exercises indicate that the Warsaw Pact may intend allotting to the helicopter certain air support functions formerly undertaken by fixed wing aircraft.'

A Warsaw Pact confrontation could evolve into a superior numbers against inferior numbers type of battle. Beyond visual range capability will be useful during the first pass or the first attack in such a scenario since basically all on one side will be friendly and all on the other of a certain line will be enemy, but this has been called Maginot Line thinking. After the first pass, however, the engagement 'becomes multiple bogey'. Pilots will have to put their eyes on a target to make sure that it is enemy unless they want to risk the danger of shooting down friendly aircraft. Moreover, even when continuing to shoot BVR, one is still vulnerable to being killed by the bogey at 6 o'clock and 3,000ft. The problem is not so much killing, as staying alive.

Brig-Gen Fred Haeffner, former Commanding Officer of the 58th TFTW at Luke AFB, would tell his fledgling Eagle pilots 'do not forget common sense . . . The F-15 is not a magical airplane. It will not automatically manoeuvre to 6 o'clock and "kill". It is capable of flying into and out of situations that we have not seen in other aircraft, but it would be unwise to assume that the hated foe is not deploying an aircraft that will equal or surpass the performance of the Eagle. With this in mind, even though you may not routinely need some of the fighter manoeuvres against an aircraft with lesser performance you will have to use them when you meet a well flown enemy aircraft in air combat.

'No machine is better than the driver.'

Air combat remains a fluid, dynamic, ever changing arena that often ends up in a close-in, hard-manoeuvring fight. This is the arena that the F-15 Eagle is going to have to survive in should it enter combat on any great scale.

8. Flying the Eagle

Lt-Col Dick Stamm turned our F-15B out onto the active runway at RAF Alconbury, England. 'Hey Dick, how easy is this thing to fly?' I wheezed into my oxygen mask. The Eagle is a big airplane for a fighter.

'We turn the single seat birds over to new pilots after two rides in the two-seater B model – it's the easiest thing to fly you can imagine. Much easier than the F-4 by far.'

Amazing; a Mach 2.5 airplane that's easy to fly. During engine start and taxi I had busied myself with learning the switchology which turned out to be the most difficult part of the flight. A quick engine check lined up, then up to 80% power. The aircraft cannot be held with brakes above 80% power or it will be dragged across the ground. There was only a quiet rushing sound . . . it was hard to believe that over 47,000lb of thrust was roaring away behind us.

When Dick released the brakes and lit the afterburners, I was slammed back in my seat with a force very similar to launches I had made from an aircraft carrier catapult. Before I could catch my breath, the 15 had travelled 900ft and rotated. The nose came up . . . and up . . . and up! From rotation Dick pulled the nose up into a 90° climb a scant few hundred feet off the runway. And the aircraft was accelerating while going straight up.

I watched the earth recede rapidly – this must be close to what a moonshot was like – and glanced up at a cloud deck at 15,000ft. We slammed through it in a flash; no gradual ascent through. By the time I looked back it was far below.

Due to airspace and speed restrictions, Dick had to pull the burners back, but there was no question a clean, lightly fuelled Eagle will go supersonic straight up from a standing start. In 3.5 minutes it will reach the upper limits of its performance envelope, around 95,000ft, although its ceiling is 55,000ft.

As the guest of the USAF in Europe I came to Alconbury to see and fly the F-15 in its natural environment – dogfighting against the 527th Tactical Fighter Training Aggressor Squadron of the 10th Tac Recon Wing. The 527th serves as one of the four 'bandit' units in the Air Force who fly Northrop F-5E Tiger II aircraft as MiG-21 simulators against line squadrons.

Walking into the aggressor environment is quite a jolt. Red stars all over the place, pictures of Lenin and even patches of a Russian bear with a red star in the background and a gunsight circle dead centre. Pilots and ground control intercept radar operators within the squadron do everything they can to mimic Soviet methods, both on the ground and in the air. Maj Les Hall, one of the controllers, gave a briefing making it clear that it was not a matter of who could shoot who down. The idea is to subject pilots to a realistic threat before combat. As discussed in Chapter 7 this came out of the disastrous kill ratios of the past.

Aggressor squadrons sprang from this and are now based at Nellis AFB, Clark in the Philippines, and at Alconbury. The 20 pilots in the 527th, according to Maj C. T. Wang, require 40 missions to qualify as 'Soviet' pilots before being turned loose on the hot 'jocks' of the Air Force. The pilots opposing the aggressors either come to Alconbury or the unit's six aircraft and three aircraft 'road show' travels to them. The realism has had to be experienced to be appreciated. I have flown numerous missions against the aggressors in all three services (Navy, Marine Corps and Air Force) since the programme began in 1972 and the quality of the pilots they have trained has increased dramatically.

The 36th Tac Fighter Wing, the first F-15 wing to be based in Europe keeps six of its Eagles on detached service at Alconbury from their permanent base at Bitburg, Germany. Pilots rotate through on a regular basis, allowing the 36th to remain one of the top air superiority outfits in Europe.

All the pilots I talked with took their air superiority mission quite seriously since they are a scant 15 minutes from the communist border. Not one fighter pilot considered the Soviet pilot an easy foe to beat.

With me in the front seat of our F-15B was 22nd Tactical Fighter Sqaudron CO Dick Stamm while the 36th Wing's CO Colonel Perry Smith flew wing in the single seat F-15A. The control system is super sensitive to the touch, more so than the F-4, and visibility out of the bubble canopy harks back to the great dogfighters of the past like the P-51 and F-86.

The rudder aileron interconnect eliminates the adverse yaw inherent in all swept wing aircraft (The Phantom II was rough on this. I watched a Navy pilot depart or high speed stall his F-4J during a dogfight with aggressor A-4s trying to pull too hard in a turn).

The cockpit of the F-15A as of March 1975.

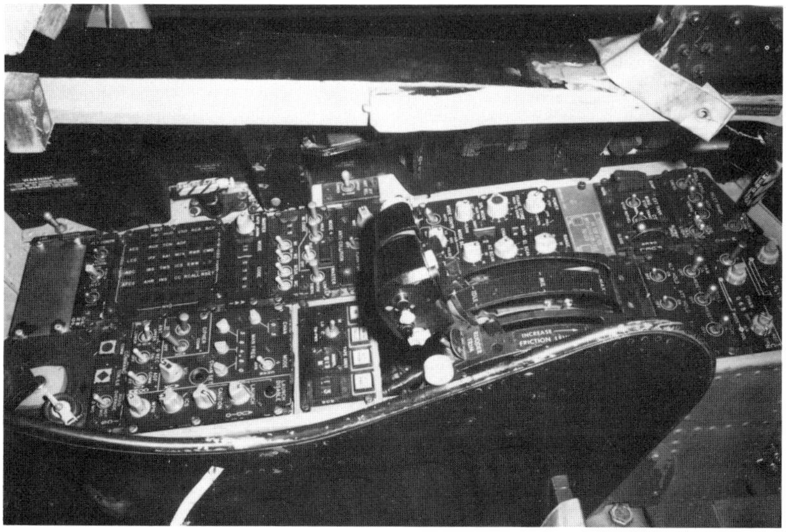

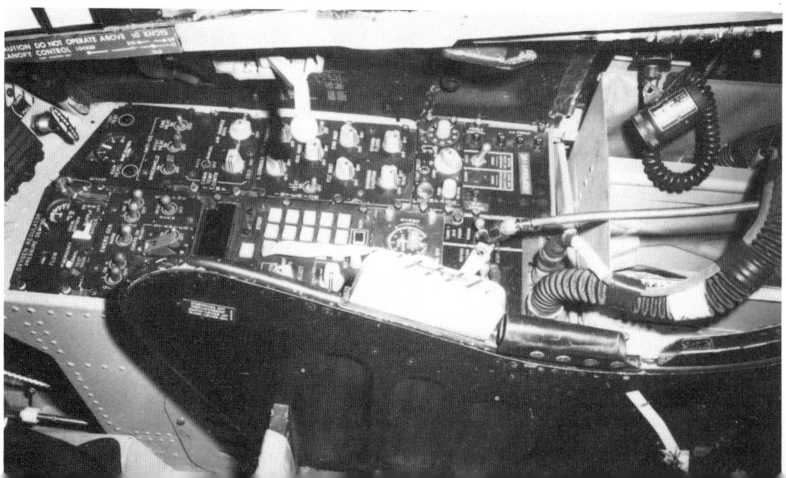

As a result, the nose of the Eagle goes where the pilot puts the stick with the Control Augmentation System telling the flight controls how much to deflect and when no matter what the input.

With approach speeds of 120kts, the F-15 is easier to fly than most general aviation aircraft. The excess power in the Pratt & Whitney F100 engines gives real punch to the fighter. Who would have ever dreamed of sustaining a 5g turn while accelerating in a climbing corkscrew.

The dogfight capabilities of the Eagle stand head and shoulders above most of the aircraft flying today. The mission profile the day I flew out of Alconbury was two F-15s versus two F-5Es, a 'snake' and a 'silver' bird flown by Mario Peraldo and Scott Saunders of the 527th. On our air combat tactics mission out over the North Sea, we had the white hats (helmets?) and the aggressor pilots . . . well, their helmets had great big red stars on them. Our call signs were Adler 71 and 72, while the F-5s were Baron 81 and 82.

The manoeuvring area out over the North Sea was divided into areas representing West and East Germany. The F-15s would be on a combat air patrol (CAP) near the Buffer Zone, assuming we are at peace unless bogies committed a 'hostile act.' The goal was to react if necessary and avoid being dragged across the political border.

With GCI we were centred over the CAP area. The impression throughout is one of extreme visibility. The cockpit is very roomy and since one sits up almost waist level with the canopy rail, it's hard to do anything but look around and see where you are . . . or where bogies are.

After a little bit of hands-on experience, one gets accustomed to the control sensitivity, although the stick has to be held with thumb and index finger, rather than by just a grabbing fist. Soon we were patrolling on station and bogies were called out at 40 miles, 12 o'clock on the nose. The distance shrunk at

Below: The author climbing into the cockpit of an F-15B for his flight with the 36th TFW out of Alconbury, England. *Author*

Top: Col Perry Smith, 36 Wing CO at the time of the author's flight, leads the way over the North Sea for an ACT mission against two F-5s of the 527th TFTAS. *Author*

Above: Low level instrument penetration into Bitburg, Germany – typical European weather. *MCAIR*

Right: Cruising over Germany on a practice sortie, this F-15A is from the 36th Wing. *MCAIR*

our 1,200mph closing speed. At ten miles we began to squint hard at about 11 o'clock to spot the bandits. No one saw them until about three miles out, which underscores the problems. One must see the enemy to fight him.

They were breaking hard into us. 'That's hostile enough for me,' said Dick, calling for Colonel Smith to go high as we countered the 'hostile act'.

'Where's the other guy. I've got the snake,' wheezed Dick as we pulled 5g.

Perry spotted him from his perch and in seconds we were going straight up, straight down, calling positions as Dick and Perry alternated between free and engaged positions. As big as the Eagle is, and as good as Scott and Mario were, we fought into good position and got Scott in the snake. Mario held his own and got Perry.

Above: February 1978 – a 36th Wing Eagle taxies out of its hardened shelter in Germany for a sortie. *MCAIR*

Fun? Well, there is nothing like being a fighter pilot for a living, but this was deadly business. In 30-45 seconds an engagement is usually settled. We came in and out of Mach 1 like going in and out of my living room, and the F-5s were being flown as if Soviet pilots were aboard. Mario and Scott were not out to prove they were better or to tell war stories at the club. Fighter pilots fight like they train and the training is cold sweat realistic.

Should another shooting war break out, hopefully the majority of today's fighter pilots will have 'fought' numerous engagements and have been honed by experience, the supreme teacher.

We disengaged and fought two more times before reaching 'bingo' fuel (enough fuel remaining to return to base and land). Everything took place at blurring speed in seconds. Adrenalin was pumped in furious amounts and I was in full 'burner' myself calling bogies, swivelling my head 360 degrees, pulling 7g, soaring without reference to up or down as we manoeuvred in relation to the bogies and not the earth.

As we broke off to go home, Dick wanted to show me one last trick. 'Hold on,' he said. He lit the burners, pulled the stick into his stomach to hold 5+g in a right turn, pulled the nose up and climbed while accelerating. He kept it up for well over two turns. After 30 seconds I gasped and grunted, 'Uncle'. The Eagle gave no indication of wanting to quit.

Back over the English landscape in formation and on into Alconbury. My thoughts drifted back to an air war launched from this soil 40 years ago. All the difference in the world . . . but not really. Only the speeds and sophistication have changed. It still holds true that 'he who sees first, usually wins'.

The challenge remaining with line squadrons that are flying today's fighters is to be realistic in their training and to have weapon systems that can provide that training on a regular basis. In other words, weapon systems that remain ready and airworthy day after day.

The next generation of fighter doctrine development will certainly be an interesting one since so much that figures into air combat is now being jeopardised by some unrealistic predictions that have not come out of combat proven statistics.

The Eagle will be right in the middle of it until well into the next century.

Above left: 36th Wing Eagles over Germany. *MCAIR*

Left: Snow on the ground and fire in the sky over Germany. *MCAIR*

Below and overleaf: A 36th Wing, 22nd Squadron, F-15B pulls up to a KC-135 tanker over Germany. Note the Tiger head and tail stripes. *Author*

SKEET
WALKWAY
WALKWAY
PILOTS

Appendix 1
F-15/F-16 Flight Restrictions

F-15 Restrictions	Head Down Reference Required		F-16 Restrictions
Not more than + 7.33g	Yes	No	Not more than + 9g
Not more than 20° angle of attack with 200lb wing fuel assymetry	Yes	—	—
No 0g except transient	No	No	No negative g flight more than 30sec in military power or 10sec in maximum power
Not more than 20° angle of attack with landing gear down	Yes	—	—
No full lateral stick rolls past 180° below 1g or above 3g	Yes	Yes	No full lateral stick rolls below 1g or above 5.86g
No rolls past 180° at other than 1g above 550kts CAS or Mach 1.4	No	—	—
No full lateral stick rolls past 360°	No	No	No maximum command rolls past 360°
No abrupt rolls above 475kts below 12,000ft	Yes	—	
No rolls past 360° above 550kts CAS or Mach 1.4	Yes		
No rolls past 90° with landing gear down	No	No	No rolls past 180° with gear down
No spins	No	No	No spins
No close formation above 475kts below 12,000ft	No	—	—
*No wing tanks or stores			

Appendix 2
F-15A/F-15D Statistics

Model: F-15A fighter
F-15B combat capable two-seat trainer
First flight: F-15A 27 July 1972
F-15B 7 July 1973
Power plant: Two Pratt & Whitney F100 PW-100 turbofan engines, each developing 23,820lb of thrust
Length: 63.8ft (19.4m)
Height: 18.5ft (5.6m)
Wing span: 42.8ft (13.0m)
Weight: 40,000-56,000lb
41,500lb (full internal fuel plus 4 AIM-7F Sparrow Missiles)
Internal fuel: 11,635lb
Combat thrust to weight ratio: 1.4:1
Speed: Mach 2.5+ (without missiles, full fuel or ammunition)
Service ceiling: 55,000ft
Load factor: +7.33g
Armament: Four AIM-9 Sidewinders; four AIM-7 Sparrows; 940 rounds of 20mm ammunition for the General Electric M-61A1 six-barrel gun. Five weapons stations capable of carrying more than 16,000lb of munitions or additional electronic counter-measures in addition to air-to-air weaponry
Avionics: Pulse doppler air-to-air and air-to-ground APG-63 radar, head-up display, inertial navigation system, TACAN, and ILS
Production: F-15A – 383
F-15B – 60

Model: F-15C fighter
F-15D combat capable two-seat trainer
First flight: F-15C 27 February 1979
F-15D 19 June 1979
Power plant: Two Pratt & Whitney F100 PW-100 turbofan engines, each developing 23,820lb of thrust
External dimensions: Same as F-15A/B
Performance: Same as F-15A/B
Weight: 40,000-68,000lb
44,500lb (full internal fuel plus 4 AIM-7F Sparrow missiles)
Internal fuel: 13,455lb
Combat thrust to weight ratio: 1.3:1
Armament: Same as F-15A/B
Avionics: Pulse doppler air-to-air and air-to-ground APG-63 radar with programmable signal processor, head-up display, inertial navigation system, TACAN, ILS, internal ECM
Improvements: F-15C/D incorporate 2,000lb of additional fuel internally, have provisions for Fuel and Sensor Tactical (FAST) Pack pallets and have a programmable radar signal processor which enables significant radar and avionic enhancements
Max flight duration: 10.5hr with refuelling; 5.35hr unrefuelled (with FAST Packs)
Production: F-15C/D – Deliveries began July 1979

Below: An F-15A of the 18th Wing.

Appendix 3
Costings

A F-15 Programme Costs*

	Original Estimate	*Actual through 1980 plus estimate for remainder*
Development	$3.65	$4.22
Procurement		
Airframe	3.70	5.50
Engine	1.83	2.53
Electronics	1.91	1.87
Armament	.25	.15
Peculiar Ground Support	.99	1.23
Initial Spares	.84	.99
Other	.04	.09
TOTAL	$13.18† ($17,596,700 per aicraft)	$16.58 ($22,136,100 per aircraft)

(a) 60 F-15s sold to Saudia Arabia for $1.92 billion
(b) 40 F-15s sold to Israel for $907 million

B FY 1979 Cost and Capabilities

	Operationally ready mission capable	*Cannibalisation per 100 sorties*	*$ per flight hour‡*
A-10	67%	17	$1100
F-4E	66%	9	$1800
F-15	56%	29	$4300

*Official Selected Acquisiton Report – December 1979
Fiscal year 1980 dollars; whole programme of 749 aircraft.
Figures in billions

†Total does not reflect rounded off figures of above areas

‡Includes variable depot maintenance, base level consumables, replenishing spares, petroleum

Appendix 4
USAF F-15 Units

Base, Wing, Squadron (Numbered Air Force/Major Command)	Equipage Month
Edwards AFB, California	
6510th Test Wing (AFSC)	July 1972
Luke AFB, Arizona	
58th Tactical Training Wing (now assigned to 405th Tactical Training Wing) (12 AF, TAC)	
555th Tactical Fighter Training Squadron	November 1974
550th Tactical Fighter Training Squadron	September 1977
461st Tactical Fighter Training Squadron	June 1976
Langley AFB, Virginia	
1st Tactical Fighter Wing (9 AF, TAC)	
27th Tactical Fighter Squadron	January 1976
71st Tactical Fighter Squadron	May 1976
94th Tactical Fighter Squadron	August 1976
Nellis AFB, Nevada	
57th Fighter Weapons Wing (USAFTWC, TAC)	
422nd Fighter Weapons Squadron	June 1977
433rd Fighter Weapons Squadron	November 1976
Bitburg AB, Germany	
36th Tactical Fighter Wing (17 AF, USAFE)	
22nd Tactical Fighter Squadron	August 1977 (deployed October 77)
53rd Tactical Fighter Squadron	May 1977 (deployed July 77)
525th Tactical Fighter Squadron	December 1976 (deployed April 77)
Camp New Amsterdam (Soesterburg) AB, The Netherlands	
32nd Tactical Fighter Squadron (17 AF, USAFE)	October 1978 (deployed Dec 78)
Holloman AFB, New Mexico	
49th Tactical Fighter Wing (12 AF, TAC)	
7th Tactical Fighter Squadron	October 1977
8th Tactical Fighter Squadron	January 1978
9th Tactical Fighter Squadron	April 1978
Eglin AFB, Florida	
33rd Tactical Fighter Wing (9 AF, TAC)	
58th Tactical Fighter Squadron	January 1979
59th Tactical Fighter Squadron	April 1979
60th Tactical Fighter Squadron	Scheduled for 1981 (supported training of 18 TFW aircrews with 18 TFW acft July 1979-April 1980)
Kadena AB, Okinawa, Japan	
18th Tactical Fighter Wing (5 AF, PACAF)	
12th Tactical Fighter Squadron	January 1980 (deployed April 80)
44th Tactical Fighter Squadron	October 1979 (deployed January 80)
67th Tactical Fighter Squadron	July 1979 (deployed September 79)

Appendix 5 F-15 Development Concept Paper

NEW AIR FORCE TACTICAL COUNTER-AIR FIGHTER (F-X)

THE MANAGEMENT ISSUE

The F-X is a new fighter, optimized for counter-air missions, and proposed for introduction into the Tactical Air Command (TAC) inventory in 1975. Its performance will be significantly better than the present first-line counter-air fighter, the F-4E. Conceptually, it is a single pilot, twin-engine turbofan-powered aircraft with a 44,500lb takeoff gross weight. Together with its avionics and weapons, it will be superior in air combat to any present or postulated Soviet fighters both in close-in, visual encounters and in standoff or all-weather encounters. Based on a representative buy of 5 wings (520 aircraft), estimated 10-year system costs per wing are $1.6 to 1.9B, about 1.8-2.0 times the cost for a comparable quantity of F-4s.

A two-year F-X Concept Formulation effort, including two six-month studies by industry, was completed in June 1968.

THE THREAT

Soviet-built aircraft pose the principal fighter threat to U.S. tactical air power. Soviet fighters have classically been optimized for counter-air missions, with their most formidable tactical counter-air fighters, the MiGs, being specialized for visual air combat, usually under GCI (ground-controlled intercept). They also have furnished their latest aircraft to client states when it suited their purpose, a trend expected to continue. The MiG-21 FISHBED, latest Soviet fighter deployed abroad, has exhibited maneuvering performance comparable to the F-4 over North Viet Nam (NVM).

At the July 1967 Domodedovo Air Show, the Soviets flew six new fighters plus major modifications of three older ones. Two of these new fighters, FOXBAT and FLAGON A, are estimated to have counter-air performance comparable to the F-4E at most altitudes, coupled with higher top speeds and ceilings. FOXBAT is also postulated to exceed the F-4E in low-altitude, high-subsonic maneuverability. This impressive display of new and modified fighters at Domodedovo demonstrates that the Soviets are pursuing vigorous tactical fighter R&D program. Table 1 summarizes comparative counter-air performance of various USAF and Soviet fighters. Performance parameters for F-X are for a representative variable-sweep version. FLAGON A was operational in Soviet Air Defense Units (PVO) om 1967. FOXBAT is expected to enter the Tactical Aviation (TA) inventory in 1969 and PVO in 1970-71.

The Soviets also have shown the ability and intention to develop improved armament and fire control systems, and most of their latest fighters appear to have an all-weather air-to-air capability. The large nose radomes on FOXBAT and FLAGON A indicate the presence of large radar antennas, which could permit a long-range detection capability. Intelligence estimates also credit the Soviets with an air-to-air missile system similar to our AIM-7F SPARROW (20-25 nautical mile (nm) range) by 1975-80.

In addition to the fighter threat, the Soviets can be expected to develop improved SAMs (surface-to-air missiles) that are more reliable, less susceptible to jamming and considerably more difficult to outmaneuver. Also, better rapid-fire AAA (anti-aircraft artillery), with improved fire control systems, is anticipated.

The FLAGON A and FOXBAT do not represent an overwhelming tactical air combat threat, even with their small advantages in basic thrust-to-weight for level acceleration. Rather, this view holds that the threat against which the F-X should be planned is MiG-21 follow-on, optimized for visual counter-air missions. Using the same austerity of equipment and internal fuel that has been traditional in Soviet practice, it is technically feasible to design an aircraft with a thrust-to-weight ratio of 1.3, a wing loading of 60-65lb/sq ft, equipped with improved cannon, and Soviet versions of SIDEWINDER (improved AA-2). Although not now in agreed-to intelligence estimates, such an aircraft, if developed, would have a decisive maneuvering performance margin over U.S. fighters.

COUNTER TO THE THREAT

A. TAC Counter-Air Missions

The principal combat missions of TAC are counter-air, interdiction and close air support, in conjunction with actions of our land and sea-based general-purpose forces.

This DCP deals with TAC's counter-air capabilities in the 1975-85 period. The missions of a tactical counter-air force include: strike force escort over enemy airspace, fighter sweeps in advance of our strike aircraft, combat air patrol between our strike aircraft and enemy airbases, and friendly area air defense in the tactical theater.

The most difficult situation is combat over enemy airspace. Here, the counter-air fighter must protect the strike force from enemy fighters while under the disadvantage of being in the enemy's GCI network and exposed to potential attack from his fighters, SAMs and AAA.

B. Counter-Air Capability of the Programmed Force

The programmed force of TAC fighters for the mid-1970s consists of thirteen wings of F-4s, four wings of F-111s, four wings of A-7Ds, and two wings of F-100s. Of this force, the F-4 will be the only system competitive with current Soviet fighters in counter-air capability. The programmed F-4 force consists of six wings of older F-4C/D and seven wings of F-4Es, the latter featuring an uprated engine and internal gun. All versions carry AIM-7 and AIM-9 or AIM-4 (FALCON) missiles. By 1975, the basic technology in the F-4 series will be about 20 years old.

C. Required Capability for the 1975-1985 Counter-Air Fighter

1. Standoff Detection and Weapons - Since certain 1975 Soviet fighters are credited with both a SPARROW-type missile and radar 'lookdown' capability our counter-air fighters should have an effective stand-off air-to-air missile, coupled with an effective radar 'lookdown' capability, if they can be developed. A relatively long radar detection range, regardless of target altitude, aspect or velocity is not only key to initiating a standoff engagement, but is also key to gaining favorable position for a close-in encounter, should one ensue. The standoff capability must be more reliable than our earlier AIM-7 designs have been in Southeast Asia (SEA). It must be designed to kill maneuvering targets and be

TABLE I COMPARISON OF U.S. AND SOVIET FIGHTERS

	F-4E	F-X	F-111A/D	FISHBED	FOXBAT	FLAGON A
Takeoff Gross Wt. (lbs)	46,370	44,500	82,120	20,700	62,200	32,000
Combat Ceiling (ft.)	57,000	70,000	56,900	*62,600	*70-75,000	*65,000
Maximum Speed (M)						
at Sea Level	1.17	1.2	1.2	*.9	*1.0	*1.0
at best altitude (ft.)	2.25 @40K	2.5 @40K (burst)	2.5 @50K	2.2 @50K	*Abt.3.0	*2.5 @50K
Wing Loading (lb/sq.ft.)	87	80	156	72	100	92
Thrust/Weight Ratio	.77		.45	.76	.74	.84
Specific Excess Power (ft/sec)						
At 10K'M.9 1g)	600		405	530	650	550
At 10K'M.9 5g) Max.Power	205		NEG 425	200	320	50
At 30K' M.9 5g)	Unable		Unable	Unable	Unable	Unable
At 40K' M2.2 1g)	40		590	Unable	Unable	Unable
Air-to-Air Armament, Missiles	AIM-7E-2,9E	AIM-7F,9D,	AIM-9E/-7G,	*AA-2(IR)	*AAz-2 (Radar)	AA-3 (IR/Radar)
Gun	M61 20mm gun	SRM new 25mm gun	-9E M61 gun	-	-	-
x-Missile Range (nose/tail) (nm)	13.5/5			*0/5-6	*25/15	*12/10
Combat Radius (naut.miles)						
Hi-Lo-Hi with ext. fuel						
with approx. 6000lb payload	450		1280	Unable	590	Unable
with max.payload as indicated in lbs.	175@13,100		880/16,500	*360/2,200	*500/13,200	410/1,100
Service	Current	1975	Current/1970	*1965	*TAC Fighter 1969-70	*Interceptor-Only-1967

Data Sources:

Air Force for F-4E, F-X, and F-111A. NIPP (asterisks) or USAF Foreign Technology Division estimates for FISHBED, F, FOXBAT, FLAGON A.

Full internal fuel and air-to-air armament (missiles, guns, ammo).

At combat gross weight (50 to 60% internal fuel and air-to-air armament).

Burst or excursion speed not limited to aerodynamic heating.

Sea level rated maximum (afterburner) thrust (uninstalled).

Ps in a measure of aircraft maneuverability expressed as available instantaneous rate of climb.

Ground Support Radius Mission in accordance with MIL-C-5011A. The F-X payload /radius of action specifics are planned to be a fall out of the air-to-air performance.

Generalized performance representative of Air Force variable sweep F-X concept.

Ranges for US missiles are vs. radar targets. Target sizes used for Soviet missiles are unknown.

less susceptible to jamming. The AIM-7F advanced SPARROW (IOC 1970) is designed to meet these objectives and is planned for incorporation on all F-4s.

2. Identification - Situations may occur where visual identification is required prior to shooting, as in current SEA practice. Lacking satisfactory electronic IFF, SEA fighters must presently identify targets visually before shooting. Such 'visident' procedures would not be tactically feasible if the enemy had an effective standoff air-to-air missile and IFF. Should the Soviets deploy such a missle and IFF as expected by 1975, continuation of present visident tactics could result in greatly increased friendly air combat losses. Since most engagements will be in a previously-alerted enemy's GCI net, his IFF problems at the initial (standoff) portions of the engagement should be less severe.

Our IFF must be improved to enable effective utilization of the AIM-7F standoff weapon when positive identification is required.

AWACS should extend our identification and aircraft control capability at least 150-200 nm into enemy territory for targets at all altitudes, although it will be limited at long ranges. For times when AWACS is absent, or for deeper penetration, inclusion of electronic equipment in our counter-air fighters, coupled with newly developed electro-optical telescopes to enhance visident ranges, should enable realization of full AIM-7F range potential.

Also operation in the enemy's GCI environment increases the probability that he could vector his fighters to close ranges before they would be detected by friendly forces.

3. Short Range Weapons - While the range, launch envelopes and maneuvering target kill potential of advanced SPARROW (AIM-7F/G) and SIDEWINDER (AIM-9D) will exceed that of earlier versions, there may be cases where these weapons will be ineffective, especially in short-range, maneuvering engagements. A highly maneuverable Short Range Missile (SRM), now under Air Force Concept Formulation, should have a launch envelope vs. maneuvering targets greatly exceeding that of SIDEWINDER. Full realization of SRM potential will require rapid target acquisition and lock-on for targets outside the pilot's head-up display (HUD) field of view (FOV). A pilot's Helmet-Mounted Sight appears to offer great potential in this regard. Although the counter-air fighter would have substantial kill capability in terms of standoff and short-range missiles, the missiles would not be completely immune to failure and countermeasure, thus requiring an air-to-air gun as a backup.

4. Performance - Finally, there is no substitute for fighter maneuverability, when evading a tail attack by

the enemy, or when trying to gain an advantageous position for a kill, in close combat.

Superiority over the threat in close-in, visual, maneuvering engagements defines required fighter aerodynamic performance. The Air Force combined estimated performance envelopes of known Soviet fighters, from the MiG-15 through FOXBAT and FLAGON A, to develop composite threat performance envelopes, in terms of energy maneuverability (Ps) over a complete regime of speeds, altitudes and load factors. Ps requirements for the advanced counter-air fighter were then specified to be sufficiently above the derived composite threat to assure superior performance over the expected future Soviet fighters.

5. Electronic Warfare - Since most missions will be in enemy airspace, the fighter will not only be exposed to enemy fighter fire-control systems and weapons, but also to his SAMs and radar-controlled AAA. Thus, the counter-air fighter must carry a radar homing and warning system capable of sorting the many signals that will illuminate it, and ECM equipment capable of countering the new enemy fire-control systems anticipated in 1975-1985.

6. Air-to-Ground - Considering the force structure this fighter will complement, air superiority must get primary design emphasis. However, its potential use in air-to-ground missions, once air superiority is attained, cannot be neglected. SEA experience indicates that given air superiority, air-to-ground missions will be flown a substantial percentage of the time by counter-air type fighters. Much effort and expense has recently gone into improving F-4 air-to-ground capability and similar expense should be avoided in the future. The counter-air performance penalty of adding each air-to-ground feature must be clearly defined, so that a conscious decision can be made regarding its inclusion. In spite of TAC's desire for air-to-ground capability, some argue that no compromise whatsoever should be made to provide it in F-X since other TAC aircraft can fill this role.

D. Improved F-4

One approach considered to provide the required capability was substituting new wings and engines in the F-4 to improve its maneuverability, acceleration, and other close-in combat parameters, and incorporation of new avionics and weapons to increase its standoff kill potential. Although programs were established to improve F-4E over-land radar performance, and to enhance its visual and electronic target identification capability, the basic F-4 design limited potential maneuvering performance improvements to such a degree that a new fighter design was required to obtain counter-air performance superior to the F-4E and matched to the threat.

E. VFX

DCP ≠60 authorised the Navy to proceed with CD for VFX-1, a Fleet Air Defense (FAD) fighter to replace the F-111B. VFX-1 is also designed to have counter-air performance in Other Fighter Roles (OFR) comparable to the latest operational Navy fighter, the F-4J, in addition to a superior air-to-ground capability. In FAD, VFX-1 carries six AIM-54A PHOENIX missiles and in OFR (air-to-air), 4 AIM-7F, an internal M61 gun, and 600 rounds of ammunition.

VFX-1 (OFR configuration) is a candidate for use as the new TAC counter-air fighter. For the flight regime where most dogfights occur (M 0.6 to M 1.6 sea level to 30,000 ft.), Navy energy maneuverability (Ps) data (see Table 4) indicate that the F-4J is generally comparable to the VFX-1 (OFR) at 1-g load factor. At 5-g load factor, neither aircraft has much capability above 10,000 ft, and the aircraft are roughly comparable below 10,000 ft., with the VFX-1 superior at lower speeds. Thus, relative to the threat, VFX-1 does not appear to be an acceptable F-4E replacement for TAC.

While not authorized for consideration in DCP ≠60 a VFX-2 version of VFX-1 has been proposed which would include new engines developed jointly with the Air Force and new, lighter avionics. This aircraft would retain capability to fire both PHOENIX and SPARROW missiles, but is expected to have air-to-air performance significantly superior to the F-4J, better countering the potential mid-1970s Soviet Threat. Both the VFX-1 and VFX-2 are heavier and have longer range than required for the Air Force counter-air mission, since they have a two-man crew, are designed to carry the missile, and must be carrier suitable. This also results in a costlier aircraft than if it were designed only for the Air Force mission. Table 2 compares estimated F-X, VFX-1 and VFX-2 unit average investment costs, arbitrarily based on the planned 333-aircraft VFX-1 buy.

Table 2 Comparative RDT&E and Investment Costs (333 Aircraft)

	F-X	VFX-1	VFX-2
RDT&E, $ Millions	1,078	614	500
Unit Average Investment Cost $M			
Airframe	3.2	4.2	3.7
Propulsion	1.4	1.4	1.5
Avionics	1.5	2.7	2.2
(Flyaway Subtotal)	(6.1)	(8.3)	(7.4)
Mod Kits, Other	0.9	0	0
Spares, Support	1.4	3.6	2.8
TOTAL	8.4	11.9	10.2

While VFX-2 has not been approved for CD, contractors have been studying potential means to transition from VFX-1 to VFX-2, as part of VFX-1 CD. Initial detailed performance estimates for VFX-2 are expected to be available in December 1968 at the conclusion of the first part of the VFX-1 CD. More complete data will be available in March 1969. F-X contractor Phase IB of CD will be complete July 1969. Thus, when this DOP is next revised, detailed information on the tradeoffs between VFX-2 and F-X will be available to enable a decision as to whether to pursue one or both of these aircraft.

F. F-X Design Considerations

In formulating the F-X concept, several major design considerations had to be resolved. These include: (1) crew size, (2) number of engines, (3) design mission radius, (4) maximum speed, (5) the degree to which standoff and close-in air-to-air performance are each emphasised in design, and (6) whether the program should include competitive prototype aircraft. As a result of Concept Formulation, Air Force made a decision on each one of these. The pros and cons relating to these design considerations are discussed in the following.

1. One vs two-man crew - from the standpoint of smaller aircraft size, we consider that for a given level of performance, the desirability of a one-man crew is universally recognized. For example, addition of a

second crewman could result in 5,000-6,000 lb takeoff weight increase to degrade combat performance, and could add about $0.5 million to flyaway cost. Visual counter-air missions have classically employed only one man. The issue is whether one man could effectively perform the standoff and all-weather portions of the counter-air mission; during F-X Concept Formulation, numerous sorties were made to determine optimum crew size. They showed that, with sufficient automation, one man could perform standoff and all-weather counter-air missions, except in high false alarm environment, as might result from heavy ground clutter or jamming causing radar interference. While it was recognized that there would be small percentages of the time that one man would be workload saturated, it was concluded that in view of the weight and cost penalties imposed by a two-man crew, and since a majority of F-X missions would be in good visibility, a second pilot could not be justified. Carefull attention to automation design will be required to minimize occurrence of pilot saturation.

The Navy fighters, in contrast, require two men because of the recognized need for a high target kill probability in FAD missions vs. massed bomber raids, which could use heavy jamming and occur in any visibility situation. The second man concentrates on fire control sensor returns, 'looking through' the adverse effects of weather, clutter and ECM. For the above reasons, the penalty of carrying him is considered worthwhile by the Navy.

2. Single vs. Twin Engines - Recently completed industry-wide studies indicated that F-X missions can be accomplished by either a single or twin-engined aircraft. However, a high (40,000 lb) maximum thrust engine is required for the single-engine aircraft to achieve the required mission flexibility. There is disagreement on whether a single-engined aircraft offers a potential weight or cost saving for the same mission capabilities. From a technology standpoint alone, the design and development of an acceptable 40,000 lb thrust engine appears feasible. Development costs would be higher but the engine cost per production aircraft would be lower.

A twin-engine design offers: (1) faster throttle response, (2) commonality with portions of the VFX-2 engine, which can reduce engine development cost, and (3) scheduling. (A twin-engine approach has been the Air Force design concept for the past two years. Accordingly, advanced technology engine work, contractor studies and airframe-propulsion integration wind tunnel work, have focused almost exclusively on a twin-engine F-X).

A single-engine design offers the possibility of improved maneuvering performance at the same aircraft weight or cost. One funded Air Force study indicated a small single-engine design, optimized primarily for visual combat, would have up to 27% more Ps at Mach 0.9, 10,000 ft., 1-g, than the Air Force proposed F-X. In addition, it is argued that the engine cycle selection should be optimized for the F-X alone, (a pressure ratio of about 18-19 and a by-pass ratio of about 0.6) instead of being a compromise with the Navy's desires for the VFX-2. Others hold that such low pressure and by-pass ratios would objectionably increase engine specific fuel consumption, and that pressure ratios of 21-25 and by-pass ratios of 0.6 to 0.8 are better matched to F-X mission requirements.

Other single vs. twin-engine issues which remain controversial include: the flexibility in mating the engine and aircraft design, wartime survivability, peacetime attrition and total cost. After assessment of the arguments, the Air Force proposed a twin-engine design.

3. Mission Radius - Major F-X Concept Formulation emphasis was placed on optimizing the combination of: (1) a 40,000 lb. takeoff weight, (2) avionics and weapons for standoff and close-in engagements, (3) energy maneuverability for close-in engagements and (4) radius for a basic air superiority mission defined by TAC.

Relaxing the * nm. design mission profile on internal fuel would result in less aircraft size, weight and cost. Those favoring such an action reason that external fuel is always used in wartime for cruise-out, with internal fuel limited to that required for combat, cruise home and landing reserves.

The Air Force evaluated a *nm. dash radius. That could reduce gross weight up to 6% (2,400 lbs. for a 40,000 lb. class aircraft). However, past experience (SEA/Korea /WWII) shows that the amount of internal fuel available after dropping external tanks determines both available combat time and available performance capability when operating over enemy territory. The problem is one of operating at altitudes and airspeeds relevant to the various counter-air missions, and the variables associated with enemy reactions, such as when to drop external tanks. It is argued that no statistical analysis can determine the precise amount of internal fuel that a counter-air fighter should possess.

Based on contractual and in-house Air Force studies, past experience, and world-wide scenarios which the aircraft may have to perform, the Air Force concluded that the * nm.design mission provides the minimum internal fuel capacity required for F-X air superiority missions.

4. Maximum Speed - F-X Vmax at sea level is specified at M 1.2. Reducing this to M O .9 could result in a possible 2,000 lb weight saving. However, Soviet fighters have classically been deficient at the low altitude, high speed portions of the altitude-speed regime.Some argue that M 1.1 Vmax (sea level) provides sufficient margin. After weighing the differences between a M 1.1' and M 1.2 aircraft the potential value of a significant low-altitude, high-speed margin over the threat, the Air Force specified M 1.2 for F-X.

TAC originally desired F-X Vmax at altitude to be M 2.7. However, industry studies showed a M 2.7 Vmax would greatly affect the structural design and adversely affect pilot visibility, since a bubble canopy could not be used. Gross weight would increase by 2500-3000 lb and dash radius would be cut to * nm. Propulsion system complexity would increase greatly to enable acceptable performance, both in subsonic and transonic maneuvering flight and top speed. Estimated M 2.7 fuel flows were about 65,000 lb/hr (vs. 55,000 lb/hr @ M 2.5 and 45,000 lb/hr @ M 2.3), indicating little time available to fly faster than M 2.3 (F-X internal fuel fuel is about 12,000 lb. Some argue that speeds above M 2.2 are not significant to the majority of counter-air missions and the 1000 ft/sec F-X Ps requirement at M 2.2, 40,000 ft. objectionably drives the design. They reason that top speed should fall out from a design optimized for 5 g performance from M 0.6 to M 1.6, and that the M 2.2 Ps specfification should be relaxed.

After reviewing the arguments, the Air Force specified F-X Vmax at M 2.3 with a minimum M 2.5 burst capability.

5. Flexible vs. Specialized Counter-Air Capability - In reviewing the required capability for a 1975-1985 counter-air fighter, the Air Force concluded that the fighter must have a carefully balanced spectrum of kill potential, ranging from standoff distances of over * nm. down to several hundred feet.

It has been argued, however, that the likelihood of our having satisfactory positive target identification at long range may be remote for the forseeable future, and that standoff weapons will continue to be unreliable, and easily jammed or out-maneuvered. Thus, most engagements would be at close quarters, and little design emphasis should be placed on providing avionics and weapons for a standoff engagement. It is also argued that to maximize thrust-to-weight ratio, and achieve low wing loading, many survivability and other features of current fighters should be eliminated in F-X. These include auxiliary power unit, soft-field landing gear, tail hook, drag chute, auto-pilot, self-healing or foamed fuel tanks, armor and bullet-proof glass. Limit load factor would also be reduced to 6.59 at 60% fuel as opposed to 7.33g at 80% fuel as presently required on F-X. This should result in a smaller, lighter aircraft (30,000 - 35,000 lb) than the multi-purpose design proposed by the Air Force.

If a lighter, single-engine fighter with a minimum fire control system could defeat the projected threat of FOXBAT and other high performance aircraft and perform the various counter-air missions envisioned, this would be the obvious selection. However, as noted previously early detection of the enemy is key to gaining a favorable position for air combat -- either standoff or close-in.

The enhanced identification range and radar capability of the Air Force F-X concept should be of substantial value in enabling it to gain an initial position advantage. Also, since many TAC counter-air missions will be in the enemy's GCI environment, longer detection and identification range in F-X may be critical to maintaining strike group integrity. Finally, given its longer-range detection, it is argued that the Air Force F-X concept would have more firing opportunities. Although the smaller aircraft may be somewhat more difficult to detect and hit due to its size and maneuverability, it is argued that the ability to detect and quickly position for the attack first is of greater importance.

Regarding the elimination of certain features mentioned above in defining the smaller aircraft concept, SEA experience has underlined the positive payoff for inhibiting fuel fires and leaks (highest cause of SEA combat losses). The other items, including limit load factor, are all proposed to be subject to trade studies during CD and need not be resolved now.

6. Prototypes vs. Conventional Development Approach - Consideration has been given to a competitive program where two contractors would design and construct prototype aircraft using 'soft' tooling with source selection being made after a flyoff between the competing aircraft.

Arguments favoring the prototype aircraft approach are: (1) Since there is competition, each contractor will keep its best design group on the project through flight test and will be highly motivated to meet performance specifications at lowest cost. The probability of achieving one good aircraft is significantly enhanced by this competition. (2) Several recent aircraft have significantly missed specifications promised in the contract negotiation stage (OV-10, F-111, SST). This leads to higher costs than predicted, a delayed IOC and/or reduced performance. For a complex aircraft like F-X, the probability of an earlier effective IOC and lower total cost is higher if the program is initiated with competitive prototypes. (3) Design innovation would be less inhibited than on the proposed TPPC approach to F-X procurement. (4) F-X requirement is not sufficiently urgent that an IOC slip could not be tolerated.

Arguments against the prototype aircraft approach are: (1) A realistic source selection could not be made without evaluating integration of the avionics and weapons into F-X. Such a program would involve a minimum of three aircraft per contractor (more probably four) to enable concurrent flight evaluation of: (a) structural buildup, (b) flying qualities, (c) propulsion system, and (d) avionics/weapons. Concurrent flight test is required to minimize delays in IOC due to the prototype portion. (2) Even so, a minimum of four years would be required to obtain meaningful source selection data from these flight tests, since first flight is paced by engine PFRT, which is unlikely to occur before January 1972. (3) Competitive prototype aircraft would increase RDT&E costs by $300-$600 million, since both contractors must accomplish much of the 'regular' development, plus substantial long-lead 'hard' tooling not to delay IOC unduly. (4) Even if such concurrency is included, a prototype approach would still delay IOC one to two years. (5) Risks on the engines, radar, gun, and SRM are being greatly reduced by competitive prototype programs and more wind tunnel work devoted to F-X has been performed by contractors and NASA than on any comparable aircraft. (6) Control of changes and weight growth, and potential failure to meet specifications requires design discipline whether or not the prototype approach is used. (7) The Air Force has emphasized and the Congressional Armed Services Committees have endorsed the critical urgency of the earliest possible F-X IOC.

After evaluating the arguments, the Air Force decided to follow DOD Directive 3200.9 procedures in developing F-X. This will include a competitive CD followed by a single-source total system performance responsibility/Total Package development and production contract.

G. F-X Design Concept

Since it appears that either fixed or variable sweep wing planforms can meet required performance, wing planform need not be decided until CD.

PROGRAM RISKS

A. Airframe - The primary airframe development risks are: (1) high titanium content, and (2) aerodynamic-propulsion design for maneuvering performance. Most current fighters have 7-8% titanium construction by structural weight.

Wing leading edge and/or trailing edge variable camber devices may be necessary to minimize drag during maneuvering subsonic flight.

B. Engines - Since engine availability paces the F-X (and VFX-2) development program, a contract for separate 18-month competitive development of prototype engines (funded jointly by the Navy) 22,300 lg thrust was issued.

The thrust-to-weight ratio of the new engine is expected to be 8:1 vs. 4.6:1 for the F-4E J79. Cruise specific fuel consumption is about 30% better.

C. Avionics - The F-X radar must provide target detection, regardless of target altitude, aspect angle and velocity relative to F-X, at sufficient ranges to utilize full AIM-7F potential. No currently existing radars meet this requirement.

Flight test feasibility demonstration programs have been scheduled to determine potential effectiveness of head-coupled optics in enhancing F-X visual combat capability.

D. Gun - Recently completed F-X gun studies indicated a higher muzzle velocity than the 3200 fps of the F-4E M61 20mm gun would greatly increase gun kill potential in maneuvering air combat. It also appears that caseless ammunition would reduce potential engine ingestion of gun expendibles and afford a lighter installation. Air Force gun studies indicate that 25mm is an appropriate caliber for a new gun, with rate of fire essentially equal to the Mol. Pending a decision on a new gun, the F-X design calls for the Mol.

E. Short Range Missile (SRM) - Now in Concept Formulation, the SRM, together with the gun, would be the primary armament for close-in engagements and would complement the AIM-7F SPARROW standoff missile. The SIDEWINDER (AIM-9D) is also planned for the F-X missile complement as a backup, so that F-X deployment need not be contingent on the SRM.

DEVELOPMENT PLAN AND MILESTONES

Significant events as proposed by the Air Force for the F-X development are planned. F-X design planning includes a two-place trainer version from the outset. Furthermore, in response to Secretary of Defense direction in the VFX-DCP, F-X CD contractors will be encouraged to consider a Navy version.

A new feature added to the F-X program management concept is the planned keying of both long lead production releases and the requirement for the Government to exercise options to prime contractor accomplishment of performance milestones that give clear indication of operational capability. Slippage in demonstrations would then allow the Government to slip the option date a like amount, at no increase in target price.

THRESHOLDS

Exceeding the following thresholds would call for automatic review of the F-X development by the Secretary of Defense.

Item	Event	Publication
Contract Definition	Failure of CD to meet CFP design, cost and schedule parameters within 10% and Ps requirements at 5g within 125 fps.	Program slip
Schedule	Schedule slip of more than six months	
Cost	Cost escalation by more than 10%	
Performance		
Ps	125 fps below requirements	
Dash Radius	10 nm below requirements	
TOGW	2.5% above requirements	
V/max (alt. & SL)	0.1 Mach below requirements	Program re-evaluation
Buffet - free maneuver g, MO.8 30,000' alt.	10% below requirements	

MANAGEMENT

Col Robert White, a recent Southeast Asia returnee with previous experience in the F-111 SPO, is System Project Director. His planned tenure is through June 1972.

SECURITY

All threat data, threat evaluation, F-X weapon and combat performance characteristics, including Vmak, combat ceiling, rate of climb, Ps, radar detection range, ECM capability and susceptibility are SECRET. Technical risks, costs schedules and general physical characteristics (size, weight, etc.) are CONFIDENTAL. External artist concepts of F-X, non-scale display models,model and/or type design and complete funding for any one R&D or production contract are releasable.

ALTERNATIVES

There are two alternative courses of action to be considered:

Alternative 1: Approve the Air Force request to proceed with Contract Definition on the F-X.

Alternative 2: Delay issuing RFP for CD. Request the Air Force to reconsider a smaller, single-engine fighter, optimized for close-in visual air-to-air combat, and resubmit as soon as possible (4-9 months) a revised RFP and technical development plan based on the competitive prototype approach.

It should be noted that a prototype approach could be followed for either alternative.

RECOMMENDATION

JOHN S.FOSTER JR (SIGNED)

Date

COORDINATION AND COMMENTS

Secretary of the Air Force
Harold Brown (signed) Date

* These figures were omitted from the source material.